Keep Laughing Anyway

KEEP LAUGHING ANYWAY

The Recipe for Countering Cancel Culture

WYNN HOLLY

The Counseling Comedian

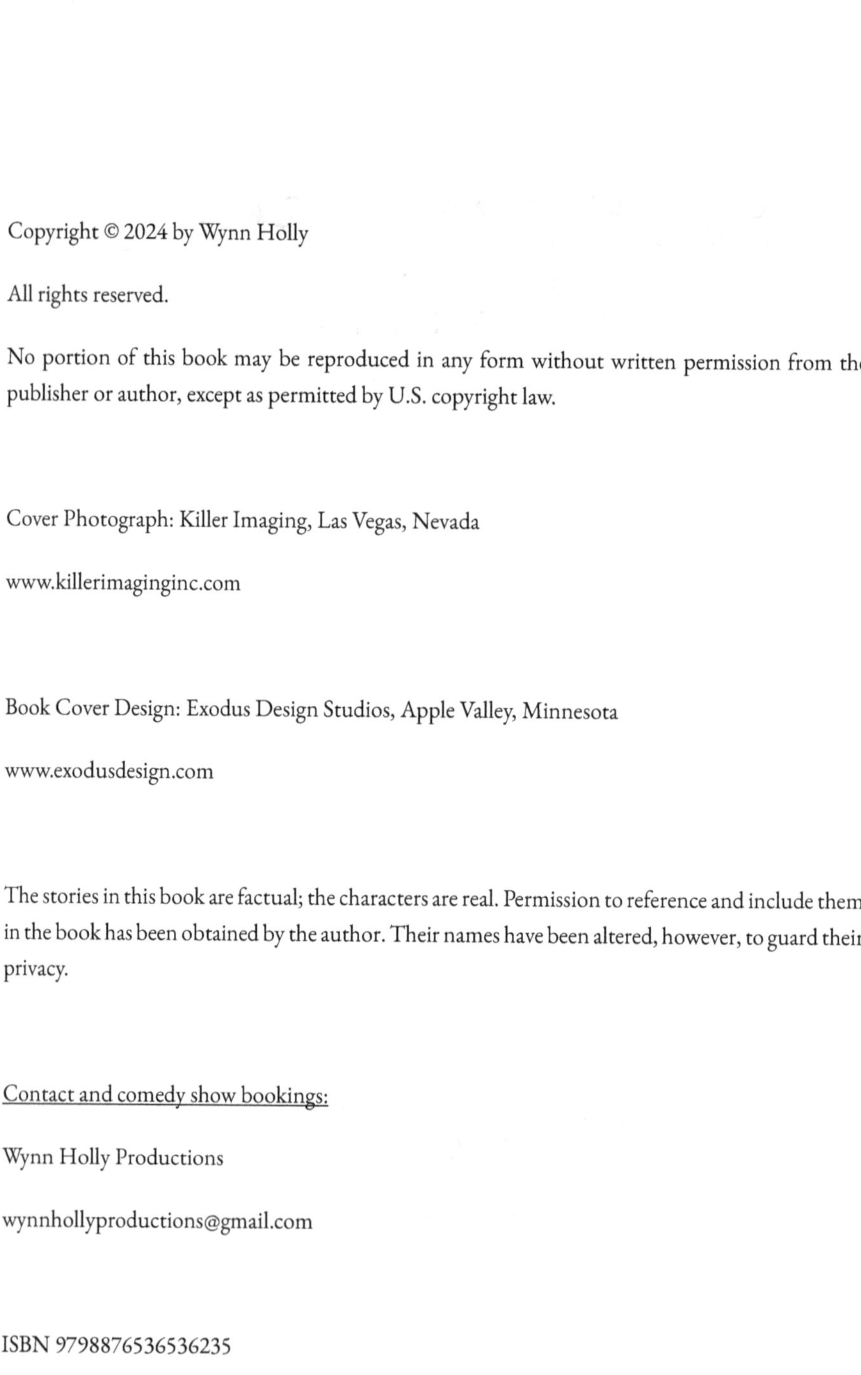

Cover Photograph: Killer Imaging, Las Vegas, Nevada

www.killerimaginginc.com

Book Cover Design: Exodus Design Studios, Apple Valley, Minnesota

www.exodusdesign.com

The stories in this book are factual; the characters are real. Permission to reference and include them in the book has been obtained by the author. Their names have been altered, however, to guard their privacy.

<u>Contact and comedy show bookings:</u>

Wynn Holly Productions

wynnhollyproductions@gmail.com

ISBN 9798876536536235

Uncommonly Wynn

About this author; about this book.

Wynn Holly's **Keep Laughing Anyway**, is most certainly this years favorite read on how to fend off cancel culture. Not only will readers come away with having additional hardware to place in their anti-woke toolbox but expect each page to entertain along the way. And why not? Wynn Holly is a Las Vegas stand-up and former sitcom contributor.

But more to the point, Wynn is a professionally trained therapist with over 20 years of experience having worked in private practice, family agencies, and education – giving him the billing throughout the country as *The Counseling Comedian*. Yet more valuable than these is a previous career in advertising and marketing research, conducting studies on consumer behavior and political trends, All of this together puts Wynn in an extraordinary, novel position to give us all a clearer perspective on how things in our society so rapidly have gotten to this saddened state. But, more importantly, now, what can be done to right the ship.

His commonsense ideas are just what the doctor ordered. Several humorous and pithy anecdotes from Wynn's personal life, written more like parables, serve as the cornerstone of each chapter, what he labels his *Life Lessons Learned Before I Got Stupid*. Each he uses to demonstrate how best to begin to weaken cancel culture's ever-increasing hold. His style echoes famed humorist Andy Rooney and present-day storyteller Garrison

Keillor, all with a touch of Rodney Dangerfield's self-deprivation comedy mixed in.

You'll appreciate how he chronicles what we all face when living on the tailwind side of Eden. Each page draws in readers with quality storytelling that is both compelling and delightful, while at the same time, offering up a prescription of smiles and laughter to ease the stressful mind. What's more, intermixed throughout are nearly 200 of his most requested on-stage, quick-to-the-punchline bits, leaving one certain to not want to put this book down anytime soon.

Yet, what puts Wynn in a class by himself – given today's me-first society – is that he lives by a pure and straightforward creed: *To show the world you are a person of Christian faith, you must give more than lip service to it; you must live it. And be willing to take sufficient hits along the way when doing so.* Like the time Wynn chose to plant himself smack in the middle of a Mexico cartel-controlled barrio, where he not only taught English, he coordinated a ministry to help women escape human trafficking. Mostly these days, aside from performing, he advises college students, helping young people make the most of life and to see that their future careers get off to a good start.

In *Keep Laughing Anyway* you'll find Wynn unafraid to tackle some of our day's most challenging and troubling cultural issues, leaving no stone unturned as he walks us through unapologetically what our spiritual and practical response should be. With a graduate degree in Counseling Psychology from a prestigious seminary, he is more than qualified to help conservative-minded persons and people of faith traverse safely through these unprecedented times.

So, get ready to be inspired. But more than that, to discover for yourself that the ability to keep laughing is by far and away the best recipe to cast aside counterculture.

Contents

Chapter One

Daddy, Put Me Back

It's all about perspective.

These days most of what we come to believe about things happening around us revolve around what we see and hear from inside a teeny-tiny, ultra-thin silicon plastic contraption. Twilight Zone dimensions no larger than 3 x 4 inches.

Our cell phones.

Only don't you know that deep inside that small rectangle receptacle, stationed halfway between insanity and num nutsville is where the Woke survive. And how most of us become influenced by cancel culture.

It's as if we've handed our lives over to the Lollipop Guild from Munchkin Land. Only this time around, the troubadours have no matching socks and appear more than just a little annoyed.

Who are these bandoleros? No one is saying. So we best all take cover ... or at least begin to pay meticulous attention.

A Telling Tale

Journey back with me to 1988. It was a time of great curiosity.

Tom Hanks was about to enter stardom in the feature film *BIG*. The country was in a good place, short of a few pockets experiencing job loss. The #1 song on the radio was Michael Jackson's *Man in the Mirror.*

Only one year later would the Berlin Wall fall ... which would change the world forever. And unbeknownst to most of us, a little thing called the internet was about to be born. And with it, the concepts of time and space would be bridged eternally. Be this for good or bad.

But for myself and my wife, back here on landlocked Earth – each was up to our eyeballs commencing degree programs; Annie's in studio art, mine a graduate training program in counseling psychology. After a year or more of going nonstop, working, and studying full-time to the hilt, it was nice to take a brief respite to head south from Chicago, our home, to visit friends a few hours away in Indiana.

On this day, we occupied the middle seats of our friend's Chevy minivan as they drove us through downtown Indianapolis, their young, firstborn 3-year-old son bringing up the rear in the back seat. Eric was strapped in by multiple cautious fasteners, secured by everything from seatbelts to thermal blankets tucked into and under the crevices behind the car seat and an occasional twist tie, should all else fail.

While Daddy Wayne was by no means Dale Earnhardt, Jr, or any other Indy 500 race car driver, it sure felt like it on this day.

So, rather than experiencing a smooth ride this early Sunday morning through the one-way city post-Midwest winter road construction streets and avenues, Wayne's dodging pothole after pothole left all our tummies grumbling, just hoping we'd keep down our morning meal.

Most certainly, Vegas had better than 50:50 odds that, given Wayne's Evil Knievel showmanship, the vehicle, and its frightened one-way Southwest Airlines-like flight passengers would flip over way before their stomachs would.

Tossed here, there and everywhere we all felt like riders on a loop-de-loop rollercoaster at Six Flags.

And then, seemingly out of nowhere, came from the mouth of the babe, little Eric, from way yonder in the back row of this live, real-time *Fast and Furious* movie simulated ride:

"Daddy, put me back."

Whether a plane, train, bus ... or Chevy minivan, it's always the farthest seat from the front to undergo the most turbulence.

Yet it was not just little Eric whose body was clinging for dear life; the truth of the matter was, we all were. Eric was the only one with the gumption to speak out and spill the beans.

Driver Wayne, our pilot, may have been experiencing a bit of the rocking and rolling himself, yet likely very little. The person holding the wheel rarely feels and sees what is happening for the rest ... unless someone signals them.

In this case, and lucky for all on board, Wayne's co-pilot, navigating from the passenger side of the front seat, is his wife, June.

"Wayne, maybe you should slow down," June says to him gently, though with the intention being that of DO IT OR ELSE.

Soon after, the stakeholders from row two, myself and Annie, chimed in, providing headmaster aviator Wayne a mini-lesson on what the seat and floor of their new van might look and smell like if said field trip classmates suddenly were to lose their breakfast.

Soon enough, the message resonated, and our Elon Musk prototype van's speed dropped suddenly from space shuttle velocity to slow and sustainable.

While Wayne failed to arrive first at the finish line and thus missed out on receipt of the accompanying roses and kisses in the winner circle at the Brickyard, he did manage to regain the admiration of all in the van and appreciation that our bacon and eggs would stay put, and forthwith soon-to-have lunch would be enjoyed.

From that point on, our venture went without a hitch, compliments of tour guide Wayne. Annie and I came away impressed with Indy, so much so that on our return trip to Chicago, both of us began to picture ourselves living there in Hoosier Land once done with school.

Which did happen only three years later.

Yet not for the voice of one crying from the rear seat wilderness would any of that occur. Those Indy years turned out to be pivotal to where both self and ex-wife Annie are today, as people, helping professionals, and in each our way, peacemakers.

Maybe the Woke, as driver Wayne did, is unaware how life-altering the ideas they bring to our culture are, but I have my doubts. And so should you.

Feelings of apprehension, God supplies us for a reason. They are given so that we might adjust our course.

Always good to listen to those deep-down little voices. Then to find a way to respond.

... And a safe way home.

Just Keep Laughing

Well, I did it.
Finally taught myself to juggle.
Just one hang-up.
The balls keep waiting for me
to come down.

Know
what my problem is?
I can't figure out
what to do with all my free time.
It's why I'm lookin'
for a new hobby.
Something like sex ...
but where I know
I can be successful.

In
maintaining the house,
husbands and wives
approach it so differently.
Husbands?
By making it dirty.
Wives?
By tossing us the hell out.

Last week I was at my optometrist.
"Doc, I'm scared,"
I told him.
"I think I may be going blind."
"How many hands do you see up?"
he asked.
I go,
"One."
Immediately
the doctor
turned and began to
empty every drawer in his desk.
"Quick, get on the floor"
"and help me look for it,"
he hollered back.
"But what are we looking for?"
I insisted.
"What do you think?"
he shouted.
"My other hand, damn it."
"My other hand."

In Hollywood,
the Church of Scientology and the
Christian Science Reading Room
are quite near one another ...
so, it's easy to get the two confused.

But here's the difference.
The Reading Room
wants us to know
how we can end up in hell:
the Church of Scientology
that Tom Cruise would die
in his next *MI sequel*
and get there as soon as possible.

Last month
I arrived home from the ASPCA
with a brand-spanking
new puppy boy.
Peppy,
I named him.
"Peppy,"
I said.
"You do know, don't you,"
"why you're constantly scratching"
"down there?"
"You've got fleas."
He looks up at me,
as if to say -
"Yeah, so what's your excuse?"

Like many of you -
I, too
came from a

dysfunctional home.
We were but a small family,
just my mom, dad,
brother, and me.
Years later,
I asked my mother,
"Did you ever wish"
"one of us boys were a girl?"
"Yes,"
she said.
"Your father."
"Only back then"
"that would've been"
"too much to hope for."

My dentist
told me,
seven of my teeth,
have ADHD.
"How can that be?"
I asked him.
"Isn't obvious,"
he explained.
"Your cavities keep jumping"
"from one tooth to the other."

The older I get
the more bothered I am
about certain sayings.
Like ...
"Those men have egg on their faces."
What are a bunch of grown men
doing
lying underneath
a row of chickens?

If you've never used
one of those
public restroom
Xlerator
automatic air dryers,
you're in for a real treat.
They put out enough power
to split the atom.
The first time
I used one,
I was at LAX
ready to board a flight back east.
Put my hands under it -
three seconds later
I landed in Dallas.
Why can't *Southwest*
come up with something like this?

When I arrived
at *Little Caesars*
to pick up my pizza
the counter girl told me
I was this week's grand prize winner.
"So, what's my prize?"
I asked.
"One of our"
"custom-made smartwatches,"
she said.
"But what makes yours so special?"
I wondered.
"Easy,"
she said.
"Ours tells time by the slice."

When you get my age,
your goals
become simple.
Waking up ...
then
going back to bed.
Should they happen
nine minutes apart
so much the better.

I just
came across
my original birth certificate.
Down at the bottom corner,
it read:
Twin brother died at birth.
At first,
it didn't bother me much.
Now,
two days later,
I've been asking myself,
Am I the live one or the dead one?

Wynn's Window to the World

The ride in the back seat always comes with more turbulence. Best to expect such. Only how do you go about minimizing it? Particularly as it relates to our responding to cancel culture.

Complain, complain ... then complain some more.

How else, right?

Only I like to focus on the person doing most of the driving. In other words, the person (s) in charge. People in charge always hate to be bothered by underlings like you and me, but that's what makes disturbing them so delightful.

Should that get me nowhere, I start working my way back from there until everyone on the bus begins to hear and see things from my vantage point and starts to feel just as troubled as I do.

Mark my words; almost everyone on board is feeling the bounce. But what those seated in the middle sections are experiencing may not be as strong as what I'm feeling, way back in the last row.

Until now, most in middle America have kept their dissatisfaction about cancel culture to a dull murmur ... hoping that this crazy journey we've been on will eventually improve, or better still, end.

Only in this case, that would be a false hope.

What is needed is a bit more moaning and groaning to the point that all travelers on board will come to realize the unsafety of the situation. And those in charge of driving the bus will be forced to adjust. Or new drivers found.

After all, mutual survival is the name of the game.

What the Woke and cancel culture has done has been to keep driving full speed recklessly ahead, without regard to the rest of us passengers on their tour de force trip to Never Neverland.

But since many in the Woke camp seem resistant to listening, it's time to adjust course and strategy.

Only how?

Well, not by debate or argumentation. That feeds the nonsense just that much more. Rather, here is what does work.

Laughter.

At what the Woke say, do, and if need be, at what keeps getting silently dreamed up in their heads.

Only with a good dose of humor will society's attitudes start on a fresh path toward change. And help place us back in the middle of the road where it is way more steady and sure.

Only through humor will people seated watching from the bleachers have the chance to see things as they truly are.

Far be it for us to expect the Woke to disappear any time soon.

Though that would be nice; just unrealistic.

But with a multitude of voices, like yours and mine, chiming in from the stands, demanding change take place on the field, well that's something different entirely.

In the end, perspective does matter.

Even if you're the only one way back in the back row.

Chapter Two

Watch Out for the Coat Hangers

Why not live a little (or a lot).

The funny thing about our nighttime dreams is that we often can't distinguish what's real from what's not when we have them.

That is until we suddenly wake up.

It's a lot like getting hooked on some dumb reality TV show whose plot line takes us spinning around in circles.

Then there are the other types of dreams about how we want our life to be.

Unfortunately, in these cancel culture times, making the slightest of wishes come true is starting to feel more like being a character in *A Nightmare on Elm Street* movie sequel. All the rest of us just trying to stay clear of Freddy Krueger.

The goal of the Woke is to damp down all aspirations but their own. And what's worse is that all the rest of us have been handed our scripts and told to go backstage and memorize the few lines we've been given.

In other words, *"Don't call us; we'll call you."*

The only ones who seem even to come close to envisioning their dreams these days are the Kardashians.

And what a mess, right, when one of their primary male leads goes way off script?

Getting caught up in a reality TV show for an hour or so a month, I guess, is okay. But it is far removed from living a full life. Any more time invested, eventually one begins to buy into all the wacky drama, leading even the most sane among us to do nothing more than want to sit there and see what happens next – which is precisely what cancel culture has sought to accomplish with their show 'n tell escapades.

Only the drama they've created is not staged; it's for real. And sadly, ransacking all of us for one reason and one reason only. We've decided to acquiesce, remain seated in our Lazy Boys, observing like spectators, doing nothing, or very little to curtail their guff.

Meanwhile, those within the cancel culture brigade press ever onward, not the least concerned with all of the damage they're reeking.

I'm reminded of what Jesus said once about individuals like the Woke, those who have on their minds and hearts only the temporal, and not the eternal things of God:

"Let those who appear dead bury their own dead."

A Telling Tale

When Annie and I finally tied the knot, we had been dating for nearly three years. But unlike many couples back then, and even more so today, in all those many months leading up to the wedding, we never once slept together, let alone cohabitated.

We were an anomaly.

So, after the honeymoon, when the two of us began to share the same bed, there was a lot to get used to.

Right off the bat, there were so many questions to answer. Like, who slept on which side of the bed? Who should get the alarm clock next to them? Who could be closest to the kitchen to sneak in a midnight snack (without the other one knowing about it)? Those were just for starters.

The tougher ones would come later. Like, should we opt for PJ's or go carte blanche *al natural*?

But the one question no one prepared me for was, *"What do I do, and how should I respond when my mate is having a crazy dream and starts talking in her sleep?"*

Especially if it happens on only the fifth night home sleeping together.

Enter Annie, stage right.

The dilemma for the husband is, should I listen in or put my fingers in my ears and make gargling noises to drown out what she's saying? And even more difficult is the question, *"Do I dare risk conversing with her?"*

At this juncture in our relationship, we knew one another well, yet I couldn't help but wonder, could there be some dark hidden secret of Annie's I've not yet been privy to, which up until now has not seen the light of day?

What option I decided on as Annie, ever so sound asleep, speaking incoherently – caught up in a dream of some sort – was to reach for the lamp and turn on the light.

This would be the most subtle way of waking her up. Only it didn't work.

Not even close. It only exasperated the problem all that more. Not only did she not stop mumbling, but her speech accelerated as if, in her dream, the light must have triggered something inside her that propelled her into what I imagined her being tossed into a three-legged race, scrambling to get to the finish line way before anyone else did.

And so loud, she got too, almost to the point of screaming. And we weren't even having sex. Or at least wise, for sure, I knew I wasn't.

My next play was to hop out of bed and head over to her side. Once there, I knelt next to her while, ever so gently, and tried jostling her leg. As soon as I did, the expression on Annie's face suddenly turned. From that of moderate agitation as before to now sheer delight. With a smile so pronounced, it would've pleased any portrait photographer.

But it was what transpired right after that caught me completely off guard.

Her laugher.

Uncontrollable, too.

And I hadn't even delivered the punchline.

The only thing I could think of on what happened was that Annie had been in the middle of one dream, one a bit perplexing perhaps, then all at once, in a split-second like on *Star Trek*, got transported into a second dream. This one – whatever it was – was now making her as giggly as a middle-grade schoolgirl.

It was a side of Annie I'd often seen before, but when she was wide awake. This time around it was like catching a comedy matinee movie, yet never leaving my bedroom or having to pay the price of a ticket.

My only question remaining was, how long do I let this go on?

Do I trust her to bring the dream to its rightful conclusion? After all, she undoubtedly was enjoying herself. Or do I try to wake her, knowing if I failed she might get beamed back into the previous *Twilight Zone* episode, where there had been only crying and gnashing of teeth?

So, I took a quarter off the nightstand and tossed it in the air. It landed on tails, causing me to opt for the latter.

But before giving her a more forceful nudge, the dream goddess shouted, *"Watch out for the coat hangers."*

Watch out for the coat hangers, I thought to myself. Wait a second. This was the big secret.

Annie was afraid of coat hangers. That's it. That's all. And there I was, worried there could be some other man in the picture I didn't know about.

So, I tugged at her arm, bringing my lovely out of her slumber. As her eyes opened, I saw how surprised she was to see me, not on the side of the bed where she expected me to be, no, but my face right close to hers, just inches away.

At seeing me, a bit irritated, of course, for having woken her at 3 a.m., she asked, *"Is there something you're dying to tell me, or do you have an early pre-dawn death wish?"*

I haphazardly tried to explain to her that she had been dreaming and talking in her sleep. And in the process, she had exposed something very dire, deep hidden within her subconscious.

That she was deathly afraid of coat hangers.

Like many dreams, we fail to remember, Annie was no different. She could not recount anything of the previous few minutes save one thing. She recalled feeling equally a bit scared and amused at the same time.

Nighttime dreams are like that. They appear real, yet we know they're not. We feel this; we think that.

But daytime dreams are a completely different story. Those are the ones we want control over.

As for Annie and her dream, I could only surmise that by her laughter she must've found a way to defeat that arch enemy of all enemies, those dreaded coat hangers. Or at least she found a way to ensure they remained forever in the closet.

As for me, from then on, I decided something important and marriage-saving: to never again interfere in any more talking-out-loud dreams my new bride might in the future have.

And to do my best to stay on my side of the bed.

Yes, in life better to leave certain things as they are. And best, at this juncture, for the Woke and cancel culture to get the same message.

Just Keep Laughing

Since
I lose track of time
so easy,
I decided to buy
one of those
new smartwatches.
The only thing now is,
it's been lighting up
each time
I say something stupid.
Three weeks in -
I'm already needing new batteries.

My eye doctor
told me,
If I slept with my eyes open,
I'd dream in HD.
When I went home to try it,
it worked great.
The only thing was
My eyelids wouldn't stop blinking.
Each time they did

whatever passionate dream I was in,
I'd have to start out all over again.
By 7 a.m.
my eyes were the least of which
I had trouble waking up.

I don't get
why
at Thanksgiving
people
will travel halfway
around the country
to visit family?
Are they *really* that desperate
for pumpkin pie?

What if Elon Musk
invests all his millions
to fly to Mars
only to find
by the time he
finally
gets there -
the planet's packed up
and moved to the next galaxy?

No pizza place
would ever dare hire me.
I can't ever
figure out
how to close the lid back
on all their damn boxes.

In the morning
to get my car
to roll over,
I first,
have to speak gently to it.
Believe me;
I get it.
It was the same
with my ex-wife.

When it came to making love,
my ex-wife
will tell you
I was the worst.
She even made up this rule.
We could do it,
but only if I kept the TV on.

If I had trouble keeping her satisfied,
she knew
something on the tube would.

The fact
that identical twins even exist
confirms one thing:
Darwin
was the real monkey.

Filling out
job applications today
is tricky.
Especially the question on sex.
What I do is to
check fifty percent
male.
Then, fifty percent
female.
Not only do I always get an interview,
employers
can't wait to see
which one of me
shows up.

Men,
never let your wife
accompany you
to an open-casket funeral
of one of your close friends.
The second
the service ends
she'll have your own carcass
down at *Men's Wearhouse*
to be fitted
for a new suit.

Here's what confuses me
the most
about owning a self-driving car.
If the police
must issue me a speeding violation -
who in the world
do they give the ticket to?
"I kept telling it, Officer,"
"You can't keep going that fast."
"What is it with cars today?"
"They never want to listen"
"to their people."

Wynn's Window to the World

Remember the phrase, *"Children are best seen and not heard?"*
This is the Woke's mantra for all the rest of us.
Well ... enough of that, I say.
The righteous desires God fills all our hearts with are His way of keeping us in the game of life. So, they should never be taken lightly. Otherwise, the daily grind becomes filled with way too much aggravation and pain.

More importantly, they become His means to bring a slice of heaven down to us. So, is it any surprise that there would be conflict when one tiny group seeks to trample on the dreams of all the other 99.99 percent?

Here's my advice.

Come next Saturday night, run a bubble bath, and throw in a few rubber duckies to keep you company. Afterward, trim your toenails, then get dressed up to the nines to enjoy a fantastic night out on the town with your mate or a favorite friend.

While out, should you happen to be greeted by one who wishes to infringe on you and everybody else's evening with some impertinent cancel culture word or action, politely and with a great big silly grin on your face, suggest they go home and take a bubble bath too.

Remind them that their vision for how we all should live works only when played out in a scripted TV show – but never in real life.

Then when you return home, be sure to get a good night's sleep.

Tomorrow, your dreams will need all the love and tenderness you can provide.

Chapter Three

A 1986 Red LeBaron Convertible, Two Kids, and an Old English Sheepdog

Somebody darn well better drive.

If someone had told us 50 years ago that cars someday would drive themselves, you'd have thought they were nuts.

Yet here we are, and I must tell you, I'm not too thrilled about it.

Not so much because I'm older, and the idea is "newer." It's more in that here is just one more thing where what I wish to see occur throughout our country (and many like me) no longer seems to matter.

Cancel culture trendsetters tell us we should all suck it up and go with the flow.

The same can be said for how they view electric vehicles, which I find equally exasperating. Almost without the slightest thought, the Woke has concluded that we should all go out tomorrow and buy some expensive $80,000 model in the name of climate control.

Never mind the fact that many energy analysts claim that electric vehicles will ultimately harm the environment more, over time, not less. Not to mention the energy cost to consumers is projected also to be more, not less.

When all is said and done, here's the thing: our having personal control over things and what we do about them – it is this that matters most and makes for a well-lived life – not the many so-called "conveniences" that get created, which, seek to remove us of that pleasure.

Beyond that, little else matters.

Yet the Woke can't seem to come to terms with this.

Now about those self-driving cars. The day one can go to work in my place and bring back a paycheck at the end of the week, then and only then might I be talked into buying one.

Besides, I like to think about what I'm doing. It's incredibly empowering.

Unless cancel culture has as its goal, to automate that, too.

A Telling Tale

Nothing is more exhilarating than cruising down a back Arizona country road in a red convertible. Picture the wind at your back and seated next to you, your best friend in the whole wide world.

The year has turned to 1996. My companion with me goes by the name of Winnie.

Winnie is beautiful. And sweet – like cotton candy.

Had it not been that Winnie was way too hairy for my taste, ears too large, with a nose to match, I probably would've joined the ranks of the polygamists, adding a second girl to accompany my wife, Annie.

Then again, maybe not.

Winnie, you see, was a five-year young, Old English Sheepdog. Our fourth dog.

Our other three, unfortunately, had since passed on.

As the sole four-legged survivor in the Holly household, Winnie had been relegated to flying solo, responsible for keeping smiles on her human, two-legged parent's faces. Which she did admirably.

As we had not been able to conceive children, after thirteen-some years of marriage, Annie and I needed all the joy and entertainment that sheepherder clown could provide.

Only one year later would it be when we would learn our fate – that we'd never be able to have children of our own due to medical reasons beyond our control.

Once we came to terms with the news, we did attempt to adopt – on two separate occasions in two different states, but in each instance, our endeavors proved fruitless. Unfortunately, this story is the same for far too many couples and is seldom reported. The system is fret with legalistic hurdles. Meantime countless orphaned and state-fostered children remain without a home to call their own and loving parents to support them.

For this reason, I suspect Winne was by far and away our favorite dog, not to downplay any of the other wonderful wet-nosed companions preceding her. Like a good pastor walking alongside us, she toiled through all our hoping-to-have-children ups and downs.

She saw our excitement when things seemed promising. She experienced our devastation after yet another negative reading on another umpteenth pregnancy test.

Winnie was our comrade in arms.

Friendly and gregarious, she could make people smile at first sight of that shaggy flop of fur entering a room. And around children, she was exceptional.

As to being obedient, Winnie was without a doubt, even to a fault.

The funny thing about her was, should she not obey a command given on the first attempt, all we needed to do, in a low, hushed tone, was to say, *"Winnie, what did words say?"*

She then minded on cue just like that – Bim, Bam, Boom.

Be it sitting, lying down, doing tricks, or politely being asked to patiently wait a little bit longer at our bedside on weekend mornings, giving us, her butt-dragging lazy owners, a few extra minutes of sleep before we got up; she always accommodated us.

Winnie was a pet owner's masterpiece – a *Michelangelo* among canines.

Having moved on from my private counseling practice in Indianapolis, and Annie as studio coordinator of a large commercial photographer, we loaded up the wagon train west. Our destination, Tucson, where aside from the summer heat, we deemed a miraculous place. And such a wonderful breath of fresh air from all the big city trappings back east. No wonder, since the founding of America, there has always been the allure to *"go west young man (woman)."*

As for my work, I became a child therapist for a large state-wide, privately funded agency. What made us unique was that we'd service families by going out to their homes to conduct sessions rather than clients driving to a central metropolitan office to see us – a convenience for our rural, often-times financially strapped clients.

My territory was the state's far southeastern lower quadrant, wherein existed such splendid scenery; tons and and tons of Palo Verde trees, sought-after-the-rain sweet-smelling Mesquite shrubs, blowing tumbleweed, and Saguaro Cacti, so many, as far as the eye could see but never count.

My workday commute was like something out of an old-time John Ford Western movie script where I felt like a passenger on a stagecoach venturing through uncharted territory. I never got tired of the landscape or the numerous vistas.

The only thing to have made my travels more enjoyable across those wide open spaces would have been if I could've journeyed by horseback, on a Palomino. Then I would've imagined I was the Lone Ranger of yesteryear, coming to the rescue of anxious parents and their children in need.

I did, however, possess something close to it – a ten-year-old 1986 Chrysler LeBaron convertible, and red, no less. Before our excursion west, we purchased the prize possession in Indiana, hoping the simple open-air, small four-wheel train-like box car would lend itself to that no-care-in-the-world feeling people assured us we'd have once setting foot in the Grand Canyon state.

A wild and sometimes overwhelming sense of zest, freedom, and openness to new adventures.

This late morning, my schedule had me headed to Tombstone, the town known as *too tough to die.* It's my third session with a young family in the middle of hard times who needed support to keep them emotionally and practically steadfast.

The couple was in their early 30s and had two adorable kids: one a boy, the other a girl. both were around the age of four. My task was to see that the children were developing and adjusting adequately while, at the same time, providing the two adults with strategies to strengthen their parenting efforts.

And as would be my custom when spending time with young children, I'd often like to bring along Winnie with me. I included her sometimes in my counseling back in Indiana. Like then, as I would soon discover in my current role, therapeutically speaking, Winnie did more to soothe anxious little hearts than I ever could.

Kids would take one look at her, and almost like magic, their worries would subside instantly.

My usual routine when I arrived at a client's home would be to spend time with the children first, as I knew their attention span would be short-lived. Then I'd soon dismiss them to go outside and play while their mom, dad, and I talked grown-up stuff inside.

Today would be no different.

Like 100 times before, Winnie cast her spell. But I'm getting ahead of myself.

Is it any wonder that children's hospitals and skilled care facilities for the elderly frequently use service animals when helping patients recover from trauma?

When my time with the kids finished, I asked the children to wave goodbye to Winne, then placed her back in the car, jumping onto the backseat, a pattern she and I had rehearsed a thousand times before and now could do in our sleep.

And, of course, being the good human dad I was, I kept the top up to secure her in and brought the windows down to no more than half-mast to give her adequate ventilation. I knew I'd not be with the children's parents too long, maybe 20-25 minutes.

Not much more was needed to do to the car, as we were nearing Thanksgiving when the near winter Arizona sun was less of an intense fireball but more like an oversized bright yellow balloon above the horizon. The slow-cooling pre-winter El Nino breezes were doing their job by delivering a mild coolness across the desert blue sky.

I then locked the doors, as was always my custom, to ensure Winnie's safety and the children's. Then I headed inside to visit with Mom and Dad.

But it couldn't have been more than halfway through our brief discussion when we heard daughter Brittany open the back kitchen door, shuffle her tiny feet across the room to where we were, and then cautiously interrupt us by saying, *"Mommy, Daddy... David's with Winnie."*

"Yeah, so?" Dad replied, showing only a nudge of concern as a father might, but needing to be on the safe side, he inquired further, particularly given my presence.

"Well, is everything okay?

Now tugging at her shirt and bouncing back and forth on her tiptoes as kids do sometimes when a bit nervous about exposing what is next on their mind, Brittany took a few seconds before announcing, *"Well... it's hard to tell. I can't see them. Both are playing in the backseat of Mr. Holly's car."*

Like a four-alarm fire, those words caused the three adults in the room to stop what we were doing and promptly head outside to see for ourselves.

What we saw next had us all bent over in laughter.

David and Winnie were in the backseat alright, playing together like there was no tomorrow and paying little attention to anything else.

Winnie's bobtail was wagging away, her eyes beaming, her mouth seeming almost to smile. David was showing her one of his latest finds from his newest transformer collection. As he did, we heard him describe in incredible detail how easily the toy could transition from one form to the next.

Winnie seemed enthralled, holding onto every word David uttered.

The look on both their faces, if we had been able to capture it live on video back then and uploaded it to YouTube, could've garnished a quarter of a million hits in a matter of hours.

But more to the point was this.

How in the heck did David ever get inside the car? The doors were locked, after all, and yes, the windows were open but nowhere close to being fully down.

I unlocked and opened the driver's side door, and pushed the front seat forward so David could gather his soon-to-be artifacts, and climb out.

Regardless of whether the person was living anywhere in the U.S., be it the East, West, North, let alone the South, for those residing in rural areas, parents could almost always be heard to repeat the often similar refrain when questioning their children on such an amusing situation as this.

"Land sakes alive, child; how did you ever find your way into the backseat?" the mother asked.

"I don't know; I just did," David responded, shrugging his shoulders while pleading his case.

"But how? How?" the mother demanded.

At this point, David began his yarn, much like a story-telling cowpoke might do around a campfire on a cattle drive, gesturing with his hands as he did so.

"It was easy as pie," he began, twiddling a small stick between his right-hand fingers.

To our amazement, he walked us through how he first climbed up on the hood, using the front tire as a footstool. Then once in place, up over the windshield, onto the roof, where he *"sort of"* rolled himself around on his side to slide feet first between the slightly open window where in an instant, he could squeeze himself in below the strong canvass white material, positioned just a few inches above the glass. In other words, a miracle ... or close to it.

The three taller people could only look at one another astonished. Together in orchestrated unison, we proclaimed, *"Geez, I wish we could still do that."*

Meanwhile, Winnie, alone and still in the backseat, looked over at me. Her eyes had turned sad now as she wondered when her newest found boyfriend might return and resume play.

Looking back now, how interesting it was that, a first glance, what seemed to be the worst-case scenario imagined – David alone locked in the car with Winnie – proved to be the best thing to have ever happened.

David had been wrestling with severe depression for several weeks, with little hope of change. Not one of us adults wished anything else to turn sour on him or be added to his plate, like falling from the top of a car or being bitten by an angry, annoyed dog (if the latter was even possible knowing Winnie).

Instead, as I soon learned from a call to his parents, only a few days later, it was like something beyond this world had occurred not shortly after I left that day. David was no longer showing signs of depression but quite the opposite: glee.

To the point that it had become contagious.

His parents caught the bug, as did many of David's classmates at school and preschool teachers. Like one of David's transformers, calamity suddenly, overnight, had morphed into a blessing. For everyone.

If only the same could be said regarding the seemingly endless proliferation of fanatical nonsense and demands cancel culture puts forth. Not to mention the negative emotional effects this has had on so many.

It will conclude all right at some point, though I'm curious if we can, just like David did, hasten it along before the damage to our inherent culture becomes irreparable.

David sped up his healing by instinctively responding to what God had placed deep inside his DNA (and in all of us, for that matter).

In simple terms, it was this.

The need to play.

David, for months, had lost his ability to do just that, to the point of wanting to give up on ever again being happy.

Could it have been that God somehow foresaw, even orchestrated, how David and Winnie ended up together in the backseat of my convertible?

What counts most to our heavenly father are not the silly external things on the menu cancel culture offers but restoring inner peace, joy, and a life full of abundance to those who choose it. It is a promise equally granted by our country's forefathers, written in our constitution, and celebrated annually every July 4th.

As to our current tale, we must ask who was the hero of this saga?

If you said young Brittany you'd be correct. For it was she who overcame her nervousness and voiced her thoughts. A bit like Dorothy, you might recall, from *The Wizard of Oz*.

Ultimately, the broomstick sorceress of the West was no match for Dorothy's courage and that of her three compadres. As a result, that black-hat instigator soon met her match and vanished.

In the same vein, so long as enough people are willing to keep laughing anyway at cancel culture and return to playing their hearts out, the Woke, like a snap of the fingers, will likely be positioned back into the shadows, and forced to disappear out of sight, too.

And not far behind, the accompanying depression and malaise many have had to battle through these recent years due to the Woke's one-size-fits-all obsessions.

Until then ... remember.

An old convertible, two kids, and one silly Old English Sheepdog – these three ingredients were all God needed to change everything.

And, of course, play.

Certainly, one of the most remarkable inventions ever created.

One all of us should be doing a lot more of.

Just Keep Laughing

Look,
I'm just trying to make it
'til tomorrow.
But life sure
isn't making it easy.
The other day
I took two steps
into this new pet store.
Three clerks rushed over
and shoved
newspapers under me.

My chiropractor
had me stretched out face down
on his table,
when he said to me,
"Wynn, can you roll over?"
"Sure,"
I told him.
"Just don't ask me at my age"
"to do any other tricks."

The older I get
accessing my memory
feels more like
I may as well
be using a divining rod
to hunt for water.
I know it's still there,
but
where in the heck
do I begin
to look for it?

What is it
with the size of hair dryers today?
Have you had to go shopping for one?
They're as large
as leaf blowers.
It's like
Home Depot
opened up
their own aisle
in Walmart.
Every box
should have printed at the bottom,
Two generators not included.

This morning
when I opened
my medicine cabinet
out popped
My Pillow's, Mike Lindell.
Until then,
I felt
I had slept pretty darn well.

For twins to be born,
does this mean
the sperm and egg
weren't able to cut a deal?

How do
men and women
even decide
to want to live together?
The two are so different.
Women –
they like immersing themselves

in many hobbies.
Men,
forget about it.
We've just one hobby:
women.

Steven Spielberg
this past year
turned 77.
To celebrate,
he got all the Kardashians
to agree
to star
in his newest sequel:
E T
The Extra Transgender
Comcs Homc.
The final scene
is a real tearjerker.
It's where we see
Bruce,
the once
famous Wheaties Olympian,
looking befuddled,
as he stands gazing
at himself
in a mirror.
Having just awoken from a deep sleep,

he has only one thing to say -
"What the hell am I doing in a dress?"

Last week
when I arrived
10 minutes late
at the dealership,
to test drive
one of their new
self-driving cars,
I found
it no longer was there.
When I asked
the salesman
what happened
all he could say was,
"It got mad, so it left without you."

Having to go in
to see my dentist
is like
trying hard
to resist joining a cult.
Nothing in me says I should go.
Even my teeth tell me,
"Don't go."

Yet somehow -
every six months,
I end up
back there anyway.

You know
what troubles me the most
about my family?
How anyone even got in
without ever having to pay any dues.

In my house
I've got
hanging on my walls
lots of pictures
of family.
Spending time with them,
goes better
when I can limit
all of them to
2d.

Wynn's Window to the World

If little is done to chip away at cancel culture's damaging premises, they will only spread further, and deeper through the fabric of what has set this country apart from so many others.

Integrity.

It's why I suggest families even now develop a game plan – one where each member decides what they are willing to experiment with to keep the Woke agenda in check.

Then settled upon, have all but one put away their cell phones, head to the backyard, and have some fun, like having Dad film all of you, creating a 10-minute YouTube video.

Only this time around try something different. Rather than showing what new tricks you've taught the dog, how about showing the dog training all of you?

It's always better, I've found when you can switch things up a bit. It's a marketing tactic with proven results.

It's also the strategy we must use when interacting with cancel culture.

Rarely do arguments and deliberations ever work.

Surprise is a much better device and when done without malice can be healing for all parties.

Just think how well it worked for David and his family.

And who knows, your counter counter-culture doings might convince a few of your Woke neighbors to laugh at themselves along with you.

Or at least receive an invite from them the next time they host a barbecue.

Now wouldn't that be something.

Chapter Four

It's on Your Bottom

Funny is spelled F U N N Y (the last time I looked, anyway).

The trouble is that when cancel culture consumes so much time and energy on things of diminished value, knowing the media will swallow it up whole without discernment like a catfish, and then spit it out verbatim to the masses as gospel, it's easy in these fast-paced times, for all the rest of us to assume their illogical arguments are time-tested and all is hunky-dory.

While many of the Woke's assertions appear genuine on the surface, they are anything but. What's worse is that they make everyone else feel that should we fail to march along in their parade, and give homage to the Grand Marshal, soon all of society will be lost.

Take, for example, our alphabet.

I remember not so long ago when it began with the letters ABCDE.

But according to the Woke, not anymore.

By their standards, unless one starts with the letters LGBTQ, it's down-right offensive, punishable by jail time.

You know what my response is to that?

PFFFFFFFFFTT!

A Telling Tale

Driving cross-country for an extra-long get-a-way weekend with the love of your life at your side or flying to some far, far away exotic destination for your Honeymoon, the two are an awful lot alike.

Each provides such beautiful memories.

Yet, on the excursion, should an unexpected complication arise (which it always seems to want to do at the most inopportune moment), unless the person you're with happens to have a decent sense of humor – the rest of the time spent together can be brutal.

When things go pointedly wrong, it's human nature, I suspect to want to find fault. Or, as a good friend, in jest once said to me, *"It's always important to know whom to blame."*

This is particularly true with couples who've devoted a lifetime together.

Over time, enough marks of repudiation about the other can start filling up what's left of the remaining space on the whiteboard balance sheet in one's collective memory bank. And if not careful, the pair that began life together so full of promise can quickly find themselves propelling down the road of discontent.

Fortunately, I was lucky to land a wonderful partner as a marriage mate. My new bride Annie had an excellent eye for what was funny and could appreciate the humor in almost any situation.

Thank goodness.

For our post-wedding rendezvous, we kept our target honeymoon destination closer to home base rather than flying halfway around the world. Places we could get there comfortably by car. And while perhaps this may have been a bit more my preference than Annie's, both of us felt, at the time, it was a wise decision.

Our concern back then, much like now, no doubt, for any future bride and groom planning the details for an upcoming wedding, was the current state of the economy.

In the early to mid-1980s, the market was signaling that either inflation, recession, or both were on the horizon, hovering above like a hawk ready to swoop down on its intended prey.

The last thing either of us needed, just starting out together, was to return home from a magical trip, only to find that one, if not both, of our jobs, had been placed on the chopping block.

We had finished the first leg of our 12-day expedition through historic *Virginia is for Lovers'* state tour and used this day to wind through the many scenic hillside byways to our next romantic stopover, nearer the coast.

And so far, we were right on schedule.

That is until ....

Halfway there, the *Check Engine Light* came on. Sometimes, on a recently purchased pre-owned vehicle (ours was almost new), the light coming on meant no more than the need to fiddle with the gas cap or elevate the tire pressure. As anyone will attest, cars do seem to be a bit finicky.

But no matter what we tried, nothing could get rid of the soon-to-be smell of hot oil our nostrils were now capturing, never mind the sulfur-rotten egg odor of boiling steam spilling out sporadically from the radiator under the hood.

Whatever the exact cause, our nuptial vows of promising *to love and cherish one another no matter what* were about to encounter on day three, its first genuine test. Neither of us needed advanced degrees in automotive engineering to realize we'd better find a mechanic, and by the grace of God, sooner rather than later.

Most days, this would not have been even the slightest of concerns. Yet today was not a typical day. It was a state holiday.

And unlike in our consumer-driven era, in which we currently live, when only the post office and a few banks shut down, back forty years ago, not only did these close, but 99.99 percent of all other retail places did, too.

On the positive side, it meant an extra day off for hard-working Virginians, especially in rural areas, where we most certainly now were.

So, I had a sneaky feeling that our chances of finding an auto shop serving up gas, let alone finding a mechanic on duty, would be a stretch. And, sure enough.

Meanwhile, the stench from under our modern-day carriage V6 Oldsmobile grew ever more potent as our liquid pressure gauges rapidly descended into negative territory.

Yet somehow, we made it down this tree-lined backcountry lane to a small one-horse town, where we happened by a 1950s-style-looking repair shop and, just in the nick of time, pulled in.

However, wouldn't you know it? The sign on the door window read, *Closed.*

Hanging at a crooked angle above the door rested a weather-worn painted blue and green sign, JIM'S GARAGE. Only where was Jim? Obviously, not within our peripheral vision.

Silently I prayed for a miracle of his arrival. Or at least a mechanical angel. At this point, I reasoned that someone ... anyone with a screwdriver and a wrench ... be it a man, woman, animal, or mineral – anything breathing in overalls would do.

After all, wasn't I who convinced Annie how fun it would be to drive rather than fly? As she sat beside me, I could only imagine what she must've been thinking about her new lifetime-acquired mate.

You mean I got to put up with this bozo for the rest of my life.

We waited a few seconds, then a few more, until all at once, a large shadow appeared behind the side of the makeshift-like storage unit. Resembling that of Bigfoot, a man, I surmised, in his mid-fifties, decisively tall, sauntered out from the shade. He was in a flannel blue workman's shirt, wearing near matching color britches, a tear on one leg above the right knee, and a Washington Senators baseball cap securely fastened to the top of his scalp.

Hastily, to avoid letting this urgent moment pass, I pulled down my window, mumbled some gibberish to grab his attention, and sheepishly asked, *"Any chance you're open?"*

"Not rally", came the reply in a deeply entrenched rural-country southern drawl.

"But I'm 'da owner; what'd ya alls need?"

To his inquiry, I proceeded to spill out my guts, hoping Jim, out of sheer pity, might be willing to come to the rescue. Eventually, I got him to stroll over ever closer to our car, his eyes sizing up the situation. I explained it was our honeymoon and we had just bought the car, but the engine light came on only a few miles back. And while Annie and I were young and didn't know much about cars, we knew enough that something was seriously amiss from the protruding odor.

Maybe he felt sorry for me, which kept him from scolding me as some *young silly kid.* Or, like me, perhaps years ago, he also found himself in the same predicament. Who knew?

But more than likely, it was Annie's sad, double wide-eye glance, peeking out from inside the window on the passenger side, that did the trick.

The next thing I knew, Jim, without a word, stepped away from the car, turned around, and had now gone to open the far-left door of his small two-bin repair shop. I took my foot off the brake, hoping the car wouldn't blow a gasket, then carefully maneuvered our sedan inside as he directed me, pulling the vehicle to the back wall before turning off the engine.

I got the sense he had gone through this a hundred times before with sprouting know-it-all yuppies like me.

As we stepped out, he wasted no time getting to the problem's source by opening the hood to look closer. Annie and I had now situated ourselves safely behind him a few feet away, staring intently at what Jim was doing.

Jim dropped to his knees, positioning his large 6' 6" frame in front of the grill. He then lowered himself, bending over, his face leaning upwards towards the middle of the engine block from underneath the front bumper. His head came to rest near the pavement at a 45-degree angle with the rest of his gigantic stature.

At that precise moment, his jeans had shifted abruptly south, exposing to our virgin eyes a crack peering out from his backside the length and width of the San Andreas Fault, making us wonder if Jim might also earn some extra cash on the side as a non-certified plumber.

Not immediately able to identify the source of our riddled dilemma, I offered Jim my unworthy two cents.

"It's on your bottom," I blurted out.

By my unrestrained remark, I was only trying to convey to our willing savior that my best guess as to the source of the difficulty originated not from the top of the engine block but closer to the *vehicle's* bottom.

Annie and I did our darndest to hold in our laughter. We were concerned that Jim, our now commissioned mechanic-on-board, would take it that we were laughing at him when the fact of the matter was, we were mostly laughing at my unfortunate silly *faux pas*.

My words just came out wrong. And at the most inopportune time –
right when owner Jim's moonbeam spanned across the horizon sky of his
mechanic-proprietor's vestibule.

The situation was comical and only made more amusing by the timing
of everything. But such can be the stupid things we say when we are not
thinking correctly or are ignorant.

Needless to say, the Woke epitomizes this it seems nearly every other day.

Nevertheless, Annie and I finally regained our composure. And Jim, well
he proved to be all his business slogan said it to be. Written in red paint, just
to the side of his JIM'S GARAGE home-made marque, were the words:

It's fixed, or it's on me.

Parts Jim needed to replace what had gone wrong; fortunately, he had
them in stock. So, in less than a couple of hours, we were on our way, losing
only a half-day at the most.

As we waved goodbye to our newfound friend, Jim, offered us what all
good Southerners say to their by-gone travelers: *"Ya'll come back now, ya
hear."*

Though now no longer husband and wife, Annie and I remain very good
friends.

When we catch up by phone, we often recount and replay the humorous
moments from our lengthy menu of experiences together, like this one, at
the start of our new life.

Like all couples, our marriage was no different. We encountered countless wonderful times and had our share of hard ones, a few even earth-shat-
tering. On the other hand, we shared moments that brought us pure joy –
like the story above.

On our honeymoon, had either of us viewed the event of the car breaking down as *ruining* our nuptial adventure, let alone our future marital

bliss, I dare say, what ended up being 20-plus years of marriage, might have been cut to no more than a mere measly two or three.

The thing was that neither of us felt the need to fault the other. Why risk stifling what was already good?

Annie didn't blame me for what happened that day though she could have. And in no way did she choose to place the event in some *reparations-in-the-distant-future* black book of hers to hold against me and bring up later on to settle the score.

There is a word for what she gave me that day – grace.

Yet how contradictory is this evident among the Woke? Blame and accusations seem to be what they live for.

The struggle, at the root of cancel culture, is that many seem unable to appreciate the absurdity in anything, much less what they are doing to contribute to the equation through their frivolous redefining and restructuring of society.

All of life (or most of it anyway) is one continuous comedy of errors. At least, it sure seems like it living on this side of Eden. It is only when we erroneously decide to turn things on their heads do they become catastrophic.

Life is full of unexpected twists and turns, making daily life challenging. Why cancel culture wishes to make things more taxing is beyond baffling.

In time the Woke will realize the costs of their no-hold-bars obsessions having forfeited the extraordinary gift of life that is ours and traded it in for one consisting only of anger and ingratitude.

In our country, we've been blessed by our Creator beyond imagination with a multitude of good things.

As for me, I wish to experience as many of these as possible for however many years I'm granted. Even if it means, along the way, an occasional broken-down vehicle coming at the most inconvenient of times.

I've got to keep laughing; otherwise, what's the point?

Aside from a mind to think and a heart to feel, I dare say laughter is by far and away God's most remarkable heaven-sent medicine. He portions it out in volumes, irrespective of age, race, or sex to help replenish the human soul.

I intend to use His prescription to the fullest.

And, so should you.

Just Keep Laughing

No matter which button
on my remote
I push
I can't
ever get
my TV
to turn on.
I've
the same problem
with women.
None of them
I can turn on either.

Neither
can I ever seem
to finish
any of my crossword puzzles.
All those
ups and downs
keep tiring me out.

How wonderful
on Christmas Eve
all the family
together
picking out
that one perfect tree.
Yet
how in the world
do you get
everyone
to agree
on only one?
In our family,
when things got down
between two -
we'd
look at the dog
to cast
the final vote.
Whichever tree
he peed on
the other one
we'd take home.

Going to see my doctor
feels more like
I'm at
AutoNation

to buy a car.
I'm always being sold
some expensive procedure
I don't need.
"That angioplasty won't hurt a bit,"
the nurse assures me.
"And remember, Wynn,"
the doctor adds ...
"We'll shoot Ben and Jerry's Chunky
Monkey through your veins"
"for two whole days after."
"Boy, I don't know,"
I respond.
To which the doctor replies,
"Come now, Mr. Holly."
"What can we do"
"to get you into a surgical gown today?"

The DMV
said,
for me to
renew my license,
I had to pass
one of their new eye tests.
Only this time around -
because I was in California -
I could pick
which test I wanted.

The first
was like before:
read aloud
letters from the alphabet.
Too easy,
I thought.
The second:
Chinese characters.
(Are you kidding me?)
(Only if I can do it by takeout)
And the third:
Braille.
Which one did I go with?
Braille.
And why not?
Everyone knows
they never ask you
to read the bottom line anyway.

When
identical twins
stand and stare
at each other,
do you think
they ever ask themselves,
"Now, which one again are you?"

Ladies -
when you
decide to marry,
take my advice.
Pick a guy
who's transgender.
Not only will you save
a ton of
money on clothes,
think of
the fabulous
designer wardrobe
you'll gain on top of it.

All those lost emails
of Hillary Clinton
just keep
coming back to bite her.
Still
husband Bill
swears up and down,
she had nothing to do
with those classified leaks
affecting the Trump campaign.
Of course,

Bill also once said under oath,
"I never once wanted to have sex"
"with that woman."
Had all along
he meant Hillary -
most of us would now tend
to believe him.

People assume
that just because I'm white,
I've little interest
in learning about black culture.
Not true, I say, not true.
I watch
Keeping Up With The Kardashians
every chance
I get.

When I fly
I like to wave to the folks
30,000 feet below me.
Once a flight attendant
asked me,
"Do any of the people ever wave back?"
Pondering it for a second,
I replied,
"Now wouldn't that be kind of stupid?"

I sure wish
I could convince
my doctor
to let me
keep my hearing aids in at night.
Now when I dream
I can never
make out
what anybody is saying.

My friends
couldn't believe
where
I got
my first tattoo.
Neither
could my proctologist.

Wynn's Window to the World

Years ago, there was a fabulously entertaining sitcom, *Gomer Pyle PFC* – the story of a marine private played by talented Jim Nabors who was, by no fault of his own constantly annoying the other characters.

A famous line of Gomer's from the show was ***surprise, surprise, surprise.***

Gomer would blurt this out every few episodes. It was his way of announcing to people he had something worthwhile to tell them. And that they should listen.

It is the precise frame of mind we in the non-woke camp must acquire when conversing with cancel culture should there be any hope of us moving their anti-everything-that-is-normal needle.

But it can feel scary, I know, for those new to the game.

I do have a suggestion, however.

To boast your courage to speak out, try this on for size. The next time you're out at a restaurant, just for the heck of it, order something entirely off the menu.

You'll get looks from your waiter; count on it. But here's the thing.

By asking for something uncommon, it may be the best thing ever. The rest of the patrons in the restaurant in earshot of you may like your idea so much that they'll be inclined to order the same thing, too.

Remember that the little things often catch on quickly among a crowd, not the big ones.

The Woke is not expecting anyone to toss a curve ball in their direction or to behave contrary to their preset agenda.

Yet a well-timed, surprise word, action, or a laugh – will go further to move the cancel culture agenda back to a sensible middle than perhaps anything else.

And unlike that day for me in Jim's garage where it was far better to keep my giggling to myself, let's be sure our chuckles, when directed towards the Woke, get heard by all.

Chapter Five

Three Condoms and You're Out

... Or I'll take 'What is life?' for two hundred.

Those among the Woke who scream at the rest of us, insisting that we should give birth to fewer and fewer children (all for the sake of saving the planet) are the same ones equally willing to toss aside a life that is fully nine months grown inside a woman's tummy.

A baby.

Or at least that is what I'm accustomed to calling it.

In my day, motherhood was the dearest form of self-sacrifice.

With any luck and a bit of prodding, perhaps it could still be again.

A Telling Tale

Annie and I had not yet learned that we'd never be able to have children. That news would not come until nearly eight years later.

But we were at a place in our marriage where we were committed to having them – and moving full speed ahead to make it happen.

We went about it like two locked-up rabbits in a little blue pill lab experiment. From making our way to the backseat of the car to placing mirrors all around the bedroom, we kept busy. Once I remember, I even resorted to putting a five-minute kitchen timer on the nightstand to give the male member below my belt something tangible to compete against.

Suffice it to say I was more than willing to do my part to prompt my timid little swimmers to breaststroke their way down the lap love lane. All in hopes of one single-spirited-tailed contestant winning the grand prize to land safe and sound at Annie's egg-nesting door.

Yet, for these past months, nothing I tried seemed to work. We had been experimenting with various strategies for nearly a year now, knowing that we would soon complete our degree programs and be free to get on with our lives.

Namely, if God willed – to have as many children as the Holly quiver could hold.

And like many married couples, we were okay with love-making wherever and whenever even during those few days of the month when the female flow was greater. We'd only be sure to use a condom to provide an added layer of hygiene.

Today's session was like no other except for one thing.

The temperature outside was frigid, minus three degrees – typical for a late snowy December Sunday morning in Chicago, Illinois.

So, rather than staying in our top-floor bedroom, we decided it best to head down to the lower deck, where the guest room was situated, so that we could be closer to the furnace.

When living near Lake Michigan, you quickly learned that the only thing that mattered was to stay warm during those six long months of below-freezing temperatures. Especially when fully exposed and engaging in playing doctor and nurse.

Yet, for what it was worth, Annie and I saw this as our lot for now, and we accepted it *carte blanche*. After all, we were trying to conceive a new life – if our love sessions were a bit more contrived, so what? This, in our minds, was worth it and felt to be a piddly price to pay within the grand scheme of things.

But this was only half the story.

We had just gone and listed our house on the market five days earlier, hoping it would soon sell and we could relocate to Indianapolis. Good friends were there, and we liked that Indy was a sports-minded town. Plus, though still chilly in Indiana, we knew there would be less snow to shovel, and that idea greatly appealed to us.

I planned to open a private counseling practice geared to ... well ... any-one who was emotionally hurting and willing to apportion the necessary fee to benefit from my professional assistance. I completed my graduate training in Counseling Psychology at a Chicagoland divinity school. Over those three years, I used the time to research, develop, and test out my inno-vative therapeutic model, combining secular best practices with Christian precepts. I couldn't wait to start utilizing it to minister to needy people.

Only, one slight hurdle – we first needed to dump this darn home.

Maybe it was the stress of all I was feeling; who knows? But leave it to my factory-producing under-the-skin well to decide right there, and then at 6:30 a.m., it needed its pump primed.

I'm unsure what it is, but men choose the most inopportune times to desire intimacy. Most wives will agree that their husbands are not the best in this department.

I was no exception.

As I alluded, this morning's chill factor felt closer to our ending up stranded on the North Pole with Admiral Byrd. Even our dogs didn't want to go outside. Also, to add to the tension, earlier in the week, we had committed ourselves to help with Sunday School, which made our first-of-the-morning Sunday interlude seem even less spontaneous, as we knew, immediately when done, we'd need to hurriedly shower and dress and rush over to church.

This made it seem like I already had two strikes against me, and I hardly had gotten to the plate,

Only what does the average hormone-hungry male think of in such a situation? *Down, maybe, but in no way out.*

Like near the end of the game, when the opposing team brings to the mound a surprise relief pitcher, hoping to squash a late ninth-inning rally, an early before 7 a.m. phone call to the Holly household penetrates my ears like the play-by-play of Harry Caray at a Cubs game.

Great, I think, now what?

Who in the world could be ringing us up at this ungodly hour of the morning, still not half-light outside, the wind gusting about through the pines at the back of our small suburban property?

Well, it was Sam, our realtor.

He was calling to say he had a hot prospect. A couple in from out of town. But because they soon had to head to O'Hare to jump on a plane home to Minneapolis, they hoped they could swing by for a quick walkthrough and tour the house. Sam, in turn, told us that he needed us to quickly stage the home and be out in less than an hour to show the place.

You would've thought that news might have killed my wanting to stay in the batter's box, but not a chance. I wanted to prove my fellows were World Series material.

Like I had learned just two years earlier from Billy Crystal in the now famous 1989 box office smash film, *When Harry Met Sally*, there was only one thing men needed to engage in sex.

A place.

And I had mine: the downstairs guest room: front and center.

While I like competition, even I knew going in, much like Tom Cruise playing Ethan Hunt, I felt a little apprehensive about completing the mission laid out before me. It would require putting on my best game face and preparing my body to ensure success.

Sizing the situation up the only thing I figured that could remotely complicate things was that I had to be sure to get on that stubborn condom.

Not that this worried me much. I'd done it countless times before. After all, I was a master condom carpenter – a craftsman *par excellence.*

Only now, I was up against a mighty tight deadline, and could I do it?

The problem, of course, would not be so much my getting it on correctly, but getting it on BEFORE everything that the latex was connected to might, at a moment's notice, back into its cave for winter hibernation.

There is not a male on Earth whose fellow southbound companion is fond of cold icy weather. He'd rather shrivel up and hide under the sand like a Ghost Crab on North Carolina's Outer Banks.

My first try at it was a complete bust. Guess I was already feeling the pressure. Before I could even tear open the one-by-one-inch package, my ding-dong had long done gone.

So, on to round two. Only this attempt also proved to be a bust.

This one I got on okay, but it was so tight that my little friend looked like an Oscar Mayer wiener struggling in search of an air pocket under the extra-tight-pre-packaged shrink wrap. By now, whatever blood had been rushing in had received a letter to cease and desist.

On to number three.

Finally, success.

Or, so I thought.

All was going along peachy until, from way south of the border, I felt a pain so intense coming from my urethra that I thought someone had jabbed me with a quilter's needle.

I'm talking James Bond, Daniel Craig full-blown intense.

I whipped that sheath off me faster than the roadrunner escaping Wile Coyote on a Utah Canyonland desert highway. I leaped from the bed and immediately began screaming at the top of my lungs,

"OOOOOOOOOWWWWWWWWWWW!"

Annie was in shock.

What in the world could have prompted this unprecedented and sudden turn of events? And like many, a good wife, I suppose, the first words out of her mouth, though not true at all, I knew how it must've seemed,

"What's wrong? Is it me?"

I quickly tried to reassure her it was not.

But that the captain stationed below my belly, had decided to abandon ship.

It was the only time in my young adult life that I had wished God had supplied me with two commanders. For as sure as I was trying to keep myself from falling prostrate on the floor, I feared the one I was currently connected to and looking at may have reached its final demise.

I shouted to Annie to hand me the water cup on the nightstand, which she quickly obliged. But not to drink from it. To apply its cool contents all over my now-wounded warrior.

I did so ... but to no relief.

The fire within was unquenchable. I didn't need a little water to put out this encroaching flame; I needed something more to the capacity of the great Mississippi.

I raced upstairs to the main bath, my stride, however, could not keep pace with Annie's due to my shaking thighs. Once there, I lifted my writhing body into the tub and parked my midsection underneath the faucet, letting the water run over my shrinking stick-figure phallus like Niagara Falls.

Yet still no deliverance. The pain had gone from terrible to cataclysmic in just a few minutes.

The burning was so fierce that I came close to fainting. My upper forehead was in a cold sweat. I called for Annie, who, by now, was on the kitchen phone (days before cell phones), where she had just reached an ER hospital center nurse to request help to ease and comfort her tortured pathetic husband.

I heard her telling the nurse on the other end to hang on a second as she came and assisted me out of the tub and onto the floor, where I now lie stark-naked. My only piece of clothing was on my head – a Christmas-adorned Mickey Mouse stocking cap which did me hardly no good. Using my right hand to hold it in place, I kept praying that what little heat was circulating through my tiny 135-pound body I'd be able to keep in.

Seeing that Mickey and I were managing, at least somewhat, Annie ran back again to the phone. Meanwhile, grimacing, I glanced up at the clock on the bathroom wall only to discover another impending concern.

The realtor was due to arrive in less than 35 minutes. Yikes!

I figured for any prospective buyer, the last thing they needed to see was some naked short, about half-dead, bald man sprawled out over what soon would be *their* bathroom tile floor.

I made out from the Telemed conference taking place down the hall that the nurse had enlisted Annie to read back to her the ingredients on the back of the condom wrapper.

"Spermicide," I heard Annie say.

Spermicide, I thought to myself. That can't be good. It sounded more like what I'd put on the lawn to kill the crabgrass.

Only moments later did I learn from Annie that it was a substance coated onto the condom to help prevent pregnancy. And on some, it would be smeared on not only the outer area but the inner portion to make things doubly foolproof, which had been the case with mine.

Holy moly, this wasn't the type of condom we needed at all.

We were trying to get pregnant, for heaven's sake, not prevent it.

I wanted the simple garden variety you might get out of an old 1960s Texaco gas station men's room dispenser. Just straight latex, no thrills, no pointed arrows sticking out from the base. Nothing.

Only what did I go and do? Did I buy the wrong product without thinking?

Annie hung up the phone and ran to tell me that the nurse had good news and bad news.

The good news was that what I had, Annie informed me, was not fatal. Nor was it such to my fellow service member residing below deck who by now had most certainly gone AWOL.

Thank God.

She explained that the nurse believed that the chemicals that make up the spermicide must have gotten deep into and up my urethra, which was causing all the pain.

Well, at least now I knew, but none of that mattered. All I cared about was how soon the pain would end.

At this point, Annie reluctantly hits me with the bad news.

"Not likely for another 6-7 hours," she said.

"Meantime, the nurse wants you to put ice on it, take some Tylenol, drink plenty of water, and call back if the pain doesn't go down by then."

"But we've got to get out of the house in only a few minutes," I exclaimed.

We heeded the advice the nurse suggested, and quickly dressed as best we could, Annie helping her poor ego-deflated, stupid husband. Next, we cleared up the bathroom of any evidence of a would-be suicide attempt, raced out the door, packed the dogs in the backseat, and started the car.

And just in the nick of time.

No sooner did Annie back us out of the driveway than we saw Sam heading in our direction. He was taxing his way towards the house, adjoining him, seated behind the cockpit; we could make out our would-be prospects.

"Whew, just made it," I told Annie as I held an ice pack underneath my pants, cramped up tight to my throbbing groin. Of course, shivering with every word I spoke.

We dashed to the church, where Annie went inside to leave a note informing all others that one of us came "down" unexpectedly with something and that we wouldn't be able to show.

Eventually, as the day went on, the pounding from down below managed to run its course.

Also in time, the house, sold, too, only a few weeks later. Though not to the party which came to visit that day.

Out of my pain that day, I learned two essential lessons I've never forgotten.

First, much of the pain we experience in life we tend to inflict upon ourselves primarily due to our relentless sense of self-importance crying out for the need to have things go our way.

The second epiphany was this. Always, always read the label on everything you buy, even if the print on the package is microscopic.

On that point, the product cancel culture is peddling has a label as well. Only have we taken adequate time to read it? Most have not. At least not entirely.

Especially as it pertains to the matter of choosing to give birth and caring for children.

On the latter, what options parents employ in raising their children; you get little argument from me. So long as it is moral, who's to say one method outshines another?

But *having* children is not about options.

Instead, it is about accountability. To whom are the child-bearers responsible? Themselves or someone else?

In my mind, it is **always** to the child.

Most within cancel culture have yet to appreciate the unexpected fallout accompanying their well-intended but erroneous assumptions.

I've counseled many women who have traversed the agony of having chosen to end a life or have elected not ever to have children. Nearly all regretted the decision. But what is more devastating are the mental and emotional scars that remain, sometimes lasting a lifetime, despite having "moved on" themselves.

We must not be lured into thinking that what cancel culture is promoting when it comes to the birthing of children will end any time soon.

Take it from me, I'd trade 1,000 encounters stretched out on a bathroom tile floor, withering in agony, to have had the chance to father and parent a child.

Even if just once.

Just Keep Laughing

What say
from
now on
we make
sex
the sixth
food group?
Seconds anyone?

I once
had this client -
a doctor,
who had this unique way
of letting her husband
know
when she was
in the mood
for love.
She'd give him
a tender squeeze
then say,
"Now turn your head and cough."

No wonder
God
could command
Adam and Eve
not to eat
from the
Tree
of the Knowledge of
Good and Evil.
He knew
what grew on it:
Brussel Sprouts.

Since
so many
are
switching genders
these days,
is it any wonder
to hear that
our pets
also want to.
But with a twist.
Last night
my cat
informed me
from now on

I'm to think of it
as half-dog.
What do I say to that?
Have you tried pet therapy?
Instead, I replied,
"Okay, Rascal, but you do know what
this means, don't you?"
"You'll have no more access"
"to indoor plumbing."
"And just to be clear,"
I added,
"That goes for whichever of you."

The pet store
where I bought
my parrot,
tried to swindle me.
When I got home,
I soon
discovered
it was blind.
When I called the store
to complain,
the clerk
denying asserted,
"Oh, yeah, then prove it?"
"Well, what would you call it,"

I fired back,
"When every time he starts to repeat
something back ..."
"he does it in Braille?"

If I send
a belated card
to a friend
whose birthday falls
on February 29th -
must the postman
have to wait four more years
before delivering it?

I hate waiting
at PILOT
in those long lines
to prepay for gas.
What are those cashiers
doing up there:
Selling iPhones?
Last week
by the time it came my turn to pay,
the price per gallon
shot up 14 cents.

Circulating the country
is a new petition
making it so
Barack Obama
could run for a third term.
Of course,
like before,
he knows he'll need to
produce
his birth certificate.
When asked if he was worried,
Obama
could only be heard to say,
"Hope and change, my man,"
"Hope and change."

I hate to admit it,
but I've
just crossed
another milestone.
As of this morning,
my
Depends
needs
its own
Depends.

Don't let
my nice suit and bowtie
fool you.
At times
I can be plain ruthless.
Take
last December
at the mall.
I cut in front of a class of 1st graders
to be first in line
to see Santa.
One frightened little boy
finally got up
the nerve
to ask me,
"Hey, mister,"
"what is someone old like you"
"going to ask Santa for?"
"What do you think?"
I said.
"Christmas presents reparations,"
"About seventy years worth."

Me
and doing drugs
don't mix.
I tried them once.

Two weeks in -
the drugs
were the ones that needed
to go into
rehab.

Wynn's Window to the World

Forget what some will tell you ... that the world soon could end and that unless we do something about it now, we're all doomed.

Maybe that's true, but I wouldn't count on it.

All I know for sure is that the initials of the only one who knows that is God – G.O.D.

Not A.O.C.

And for my money, I'm glad the former oversees things, not the other way around.

As for having or adopting children, I will tell you this; They are the best thing ever.

Making my advice to newlyweds and child-bearing couples simple – disregard what cancel culture has in mind who'd prefer you minimize that joy.

Have as many kids as you deem fit. They are the best reward you'll ever receive for having made it in one piece to adulthood.

Better even than winning *Final Jeopardy*.

Chapter Six

"B"

...Then God made man. Oops.

Gadzooks!

The justification of late for everything the Woke dreams up is that if it seems remotely plausible, it must be okay to implement even when common sense would deem otherwise.

You see it everywhere – be it the legalization of marijuana, the passing over in the prosecution of crime, abortion on demand, or even the recent trend of toying around the edges with the acceptance these days of pedophilia.

Oh, and let's not forget this one – instructing kindergartners about transgenderism.

The list increases with each passing month.

What cancel culture has failed to realize is that you can't go against the universe's one overriding fundamental law; that for every action, there will be, by default, a complementary reaction. And, at that, often a significant negative consequence to go along with it, stepping front and center in its place.

This axiom holds, even in our own lives, with the small stuff we might from time to time, entertain doing. How is it that humans seem constantly to want to shoot themselves in the foot?

The simplest of our actions can have notable repercussions. Is it too far removed to suggest that when God first made us, He may have had for a minute or two ....

... Some second thoughts?

A Telling Tale

What would make two of the most miniature people on the planet choose to fork out good money, buy, and then raise one of the most enormous dogs known to man?

I suspect it is probably the same reason couples often marry those who are opposite of them; it provides balance and makes one feel more substantial.

As to our being a married couple, Annie and I were complete opposites. Aside from our religious faith, we had only one common denominator: our pint-size human frames. Both of us were relatively tiny for our respective sexes. Even with her shoes on, Annie barely tipped the charts at five feet; I, on the other hand, had little to brag about either, being only a few inches taller. Neither of us weighed much more than a Chihuahua.

So, the day we brought home a Saint Bernard puppy into our upper Midwestern home, it was an unbelievable surprise to all our many family members and friends.

While we were never quite sure just how big our saint among saints might grow up to be, one thing we knew for certain. As sure as picnic flies are destined to show up at an outdoor church social, our newborn, four-legged baby boy would surpass us by circumference, girth, and height.

And grow he did, to nearly 200 pounds in under a year.

When he first entered our lives, he was puny enough that even Annie could cradle him in her arms at just under nine weeks old.

But what now to name him? That was the big question facing us. What would be fitting for this slobbering Swiss Alps transplant to wheat field Illinois? For nearly two weeks, we went round and round on names.

That is, until one Monday, it made perfect sense.

It was wintertime in Chicago in the mid-1980s, just one year after the famed Super Bowl Shuffling Chicago Bears won all the marbles in Super Bowl XX. We were glued to our TV set this ABC Monday Night Football evening, watching another game played at downtown lakefront Soldier Field.

Outside our window and inside the stadium, the snow was coming down in batches, the wind doing its job admirably, which gave Chicago the nickname *The Windy City.*

It was a close contest, and like the year before, Coach Ditka was up to his usual tricks late in the game. The Bears had the ball near the end zone, and like the previous season, he'd sometimes like to change things up and put defensive tackle William "Refrigerator" Perry in at fullback.

All 335 pounds of him.

Like a snowplow truck, easily pushing away a mountain of the white stuff, Perry could do the same with any manned defensive obstacle standing in his way. At the two-and-three-foot line, there was just no stopping him. So long as he held onto the ball, which he did most of the time. The guy was as powerful as a Nor'easter New England blizzard.

Just as Perry crossed the goal line for yet another in a series of what indeed must've been record-breaking points scored by a defensive lineman, it was then that it hit us.

All at once, Annie and I shouted, *"Let's name our little saint Blizzard."*

The next few months or so, as he blew through his teen dog years, Blizzard resembled more of a big galoot. His legs would spread out from all directions when he ran, ears flopping uncontrollably, and a tongue the size of a hippo, tangling this way and that from his enormous gums.

Soon enough, though, he became a "man." Those awkward-looking teenage muscles and bones took flight.

His stature was immense, and his strength notable. As to his temperament, Blizzard always remained lovable and gentle. He was the total embodiment of a WWE champion. A Hulk Hogan, only with a nearly three-foot-long tail, flipping and flying behind him.

When Annie and I would take him out for a stroll through the neighborhood or to the park for a walk, all eyes were on him.

... And so, too, now on us.

For two unnoticeable, unassuming people meandering through their early adult years, where our voices often would go unregistered because of our itsy bitsy size, this was a whole new ball game. For now, in the company of Blizzard, all at once, everything changed.

People we didn't know would approach us, intending to say hi and meet this giant tamed bear-like beast. You'd have thought we had just won the Illinois State Lottery by the swarm of onlookers surrounding us.

Suddenly *our* size didn't seem to matter much any longer. The fact that two such microcosms of the human form had the oomph to put a leash on the USA's version of the African Savanna Elephant spoke volumes.

In the presence of Blizzard, or "B", as we'd soon begin calling him, we were a force now to be reckoned with.

It was almost as if Annie and I had gotten from B a blood transfusion, Blizzard serving as the donor, and us, his human parents, the donees. Instantaneously, we became more powerful and courageous, possessing extraordinary fortitude.

Vicariously, we felt encouraged to rise above our shame-felt smallness and respond like the people God had all along intended for Annie and me to be. Individuals saved by His grace, having an eternal destiny, uniquely blessed with a *Holy Spirit* giving us the power to fend off any obstacle we might encounter down here on ill-infested Earth.

So, when our very healthy polar bear-sized comrade suddenly died of kidney failure even before he reached the ripe old age of seven years, I cried more than ever. And so did Annie.

She would tell you I was nearly inconsolable. Blizzard had been the proud son I never had (or would ever have) and the father I most imagined wanting to grow up having. He represented both playmate and protector in one humongous package.

It took months and months of plowing through the grief process, but over time, my mourning subsided, and I began to recall all the joy Blizzard brought into my life.

Especially the funnier moments we had together.

For instance, B loved playing hide 'n seek in the backyard with human daddy. Little did he realize there was no tall bush or tree trunk broad enough to shield his massive King Kong-like dimensions.

But we'd play anyway.

He'd start first and hide. Then I would hide, which was ridiculous, given all dogs' ability to detect anything they have an inkling to sniff out. My only wish was that strapped around his neck would be a barrel of brandy or at least a mixing brew of some Swiss-German-made ale when he eventually found me.

Another game Blizzard and I liked to play in our January snow-packed northwest suburb backyard was tackle football.

He must've figured out how the game was played by watching his hero, the *Frig,* do his thing each time we caught the Bears on TV. Saint Bernards might appear dumb, but they are remarkably intelligent.

B would pick up the white-striped pigskin with his teeth by its laces, maneuver it deeper inside his mouth, using his massive jowls to hold it, then take off fast through the 7-9 inches of fresh snow. I'd follow suit, chasing from behind after him like some desperate Green Bay Packers cornerback, just praying I could prevent him from crossing the goal line.

He'd let me catch up to him in time, only to humor me. And just as if Blizzard was Walter Payton himself, for me to tackle him, I'd be forced to dive forward, flying across the air like an eagle, reaching my arms out to intercept him before he made his way for a touchdown between the two giant maple trees serving as goal post in the front yard.

There just wasn't much B and I couldn't do together.

He was too big to hurt.

He was a gladiator.

Our gladiator.

On more than one occasion, he prevented a would-be home invasion intruder from even thinking about further trying it.

And about Annie, for Blizzard, she was his mommy.

So, it was not uncommon and understandable that he'd be constantly on the lookout for any potential threat to her, which we suspect brought on his early demise.

It was a day in early spring. By then, we were living in Indianapolis and had recently moved from a house we had been renting into a home we had purchased.

Not only were the surroundings and people new to us, but they were also for Blizzard, stationing him on high alert.

To fend off a perceived hostile situation, *"Blizz,"* another nickname we liked using for him, bit into what he imagined was a would-be-perpetrator, not forcefully, mind you, but more as a simple warning: don't cross the picket line where Mommy is until I know for sure I can trust you. Blizzard was aware of his mammoth power and favor over any competitor.

Yet that small, barely-breaking-the-skin bite did its job. Not so much on the person, but on B. In only a matter of a day or two, Blizz became gravely ill.

Our vet surmised that small traces of infected germs from underneath the torn skin of the one B gripped his mouth around found a way into Blizzard's bloodstream. Then, once in, the festering anti-white blood cell enemy made its voyage onto his major internal organs. An infection took root and later developed into full-fledged kidney failure.

Almost as a matter of course, as saints were bred to do from ancient times, B gave his life for the one he loved most, with little thought or strategizing about it. It's what the animal world does.

Instinctively animals defend. Primarily to protect either one of two things: their territory or its' young.

Similarly, there is a battle waging in this country for territorial occupation and child domination.

It may not rise to the level of a world war, a civil war, or a quasi-military conflict. But it is infecting many just the same. Much of the fabric of what America has traditionally been about is dissolving before our eyes.

Hands raised high in worship throughout local churches will not deter the advancement of cancel culture. Other tools, complementary to prayer and supplication, are necessary.

Who's providing you with the strength to choose to make a difference?

Is there a B in your life, someone calling you to press forward?

If it is not your children or grandchildren, it should be. Is it not for their sake that we do most things? They give our lives real purpose and inspire us to be better *and* do better.

The pressing question in front of us who are non-woke is, will there be anything left of value to pass on to those we love? Do not for a second think that this is not cancel culture's goal.

But there are ways to stem the tide. Which leads me to a more pertinent question.

When will we lose our fear of contradicting counter-culture?

Keep Laughing Anyway makes for a good start on how, when, and where to push back – a powerful one. You would not have stayed with this book this long had you not felt this was the case.

Bad ideas deserve to be laughed at. Laughter alone can generate a retreat by those bent on imposing their will upon well-established, fortified boundaries.

How?

By making ideas that are destructive decrease in proportion to those that hold far greater merit.

Yet better it is, in the long game, to think of ourselves as Refrigerator Perry or like Annie's and my "B".

Something that says:

"I'm big, worthwhile, and loveable.
But most of all – unstoppable."

Just Keep Laughing

I
let my
tattoo artist
talk me
into inking
his latest drawing on me:
One inch
above my left eyelid -
Of a sensational-looking woman.
But oh, what a mistake.
All week long
my right eye's
been going cross-eyed,
trying to sneak a peek.

In my house
I've got these two
identical-looking sliding glass doors.
One
steps me out of the shower,
the other
out to the barbecue
in the backyard.
Neighbors sell tickets,

whenever
I get
the two
confused.

Of course,
God's in favor of gambling.
How do I know?
In the Bible
He tells us
to give
10 percent back
to our local church.

At church services
last Sunday,
people everywhere
stood waving their hands up in the air.
Looking down,
I could only imagine
what God
had to be thinking:
Why are there so many questions?

Once
God
finished creating the Earth,
next
He made man.
Hey,
even God's
entitled to
one mistake.

When I was
19 and crazy
all I wished for
was to get laid.
Now
that I'm older is
will I have a nice view
from whatever cemetery plot
they stick me in.
What is it about
men's fascination
on wanting always
to be horizontal?

Of course,
I'm for social justice.
It's why I believe

everyone
at least once
should be made to buy furniture
from IKEA,
then
be forced to assemble
that damn crap
themselves.

As a comedian
to make ends meet,
sometimes
I've got to apply for part-time jobs.
What's hard
is having to answer
the question on sex.
Once on one application
I was given three choices:
Male,
Female,
or
Wait and decide later.
I went with number three.
Who knows?
Come tomorrow morning,
maybe I'll like the idea
from now on of
peeing sitting down.

Last night,
when I got home
I caught my cat
Millie
in bed with three of her tomboys.
"Hey, what gives?"
I demanded.
"How do you expect me"
"to feed all of you on what little I make?"
"Don't worry,"
Millie answered.
"Ralph and Sam here on my left,"
"They're vegetarians."

All I can figure
is that I must have
some troubled relative
I don't know about
who works
down at the IRS.
How else
do I explain
year after year,
sending them
all my money?

When it comes to
electing someone
for President,
I'm for
anyone
capable of speaking
their own mind.
... Or
did I just
identify
our current problem?

Wynn's Window to the World

Most weeks, the most challenging thing I face is simply training my mind to think before I act – especially when the pace of the world moves at lightning speed.

The Woke loves it this way.

They know that a fast pace gives them the upper hand in winning over the culture's mindset. Far be it for them to desire people to be given time to think through all the many repercussions of their harmful claims and passive-aggressive undertakings.

It's harder to hit a 100-mph fastball than a slow lop.

Nevertheless, for me and all the others who've been sitting on the bench in the non-woke dugout, it's high time to prepare to step up to the plate. While I'm not quite sure what inning we're in, but rest assured, it's beyond the seventh inning stretch.

In other words, time to make our voices known.

Or at least our laughter.

The security and sanity of those we care most about along with their future is riding on it.

Our children.

If you're a bit skittish about getting out on the field and moving forward, there is a plan B.

Get yourself your own 200-pound Saint Bernard, and let him do most of the talking for you.

Works 99.99% of the time.

Chapter Seven

Love is ....

Fill'er up.

Isn't it amazing – what we tend to fill up our lives with?

This thing, that thing, the other thing.

Yet the one thing that confuses me the most is the proliferation of tattoos we've come to see in recent years.

Over one-third of Americans unabashedly now have at least one; many have on them more than a dozen. Over one-half of millennials under forty wear them with pride – a total of roughly 38 million individuals.

However you slice it, that's a colossal Crayola box bundle of colors.

While the rush to head to your local tattoo shop to acquire the latest work of art can not be solely attributed to cancel culture, nevertheless, for almost all who sport them, many will tell you these symbolize something beyond the intention simply to express one's unique personality.

I liken them to a previous era, that of the tumultuous 1960s, when what occurred was an outright mass attack on traditionalism and where today's cancel culture madness was first conceived. Tattoos symbolize and reflect much that same attitude today. Though their statements are way quieter, still, many who collect them are, on one level or another, arguing for a juxtaposition from long-established underpinnings and values.

Like registered trademarks, each person's skin is a testimony unto itself.

As for me I can't help but think of them as resembling oversized Post-it notes – aids to help people remember stuff.

Only not as sticky notes placed, as usual, somewhere on a desk at home or the office but instead carved out on the various nooks and crannies of one's body, like an archeological petroglyph, spelling out some hidden meaning to be deciphered by the owner and a would-be passersby.

I can only assume those who have them permanently inked onto their skin do it to remind themselves of something as well – a place, a time, or someone important that they want to be sure equally to never forget. My only thought is ... could not folks have chosen a more leisurely, less painful way?

Ouch!

A Telling Tale

One's tattoos certainly tell us something about a person's thoughts, ideas and feelings, but fall way short of exposing that part of them that underneath motivates their very being.

Love.

It is the very essence for why we even exist, is it not? To be free to give it as well as to receive it, these are the experiences that make life truly worthwhile.

Nowhere is this more fully demonstrated than when two people connect on a spiritual level and fall in love.

The truth is, however, when it comes to *being* in love, sometimes it works out, and sometimes it doesn't.

We've all been there. Some of us have been in love a few times, some more than a few.

Whichever the case may be, so much success in a romance's longevity depends on stuff outside of one's control, which makes *staying* in love all the more challenging. It's an uphill battle from the get-go – even if all the stars are aligned in one's favor.

Speaking as a counselor, I find it astonishing that couples manage to stay married for five years, let alone fifty. This is true even when the two spouses possess strong religious beliefs. While certainly not desired by our heavenly father marital disunion is a fact of life.

After a twenty-plus-year marriage with Annie, when it happened that we divorced, it was tough on both of us.

Saying goodbye is never easy. Still, due to the pull and need for emotional bonding, like Carly Simon once sang about, we just can't keep it from *coming around again.*

For me, when I was able emotionally to move on, my love interests fell to two women, both Hispanic. The second one I met while in Mexico teaching English (my story on her comes later in chapter 9).

The first one, however, was a woman I met in Los Angeles, a USA resident but originally from Costa Rica.

For *Gringo* males, like myself, this is what eventually happens when you live long enough in the far southwestern corner of our majestic country, where the proliferation of Latinos, in recent years, has grown exponentially.

Soon enough, we find ourselves enamored with Spanish culture, and it's not just the food. It's *everything:* the music, the emphasis on family, devotion to faith, and a focus on solid values. I've often commented to my more-than-white friends back east who have little knowledge or first-hand experience of the Spanish way that it is a rich culture, intensely aromatic.

Hypnotic, even.

And when it comes to Latina women, good gracious, it's all too easy to become mesmerized. And once achieved, should the circumstances be right, you find yourself falling in love with one.

Or as I indicated, in my case, two.

Ask almost any heart-pounding male, and he will tell you the same. There exists some magnetic pull, like positively charged ions, that radiate off the Spanish femenina. Their bewitching allure soon captures the soul of any guy who dares draw within striking distance of her spell-bounding web.

I first met my *"Tica"* on one of my comedy-writing assignments in LA. This is what women from Costa Rica are commonly called. The term translated loosely refers to their friendly dispositions – a wonderful blend of openness and warmth.

My time spent with her in the City of Angels, I found, to be a pleasant diversion, but as for where I called home at the time, my liking gravitated towards the nearby desert, in Palm Springs, where the sun shone brightly for some 350 days of the year.

The two of us hit it off almost instantly – her name: was Sobella. She was small-framed, possessing a magnificent smile. Still, her eyes spoke of exceeding mischief.

As for what she found attractive about me, God only knows.

Maybe it was my Frank Sinatra-like aqua eyes – an extraordinarily uncommon occurrence found on only the rarest among males born anywhere south of the US border. But I suspect, too, it was my gentleness, mutual respect for others, and a wacky sense of humor. Though all three, I'm sure, were a distant second to my baby blues.

After only a few short weeks of getting acquainted, we began getting together more regularly.

Consequently, as you might guess, my "writing" activities magically increased. Or at least that's what I kept telling myself and her. I couldn't wait for the end of the week when I knew Friday night I'd pack an overnight bag and head towards the Pacific, having the chance to spend time with my newfound best friend.

While never forgetting Annie, I was glad to be spending time with Sobella. Even writing her name now, I still get goosebumps.

As to activities, more times than not, we enjoyed just hanging out. We'd go shopping, grab a bite to eat, and visit with her friends. Sunday morning we would attend church before I needed to rush back home later that afternoon to prepare for another work week. Nothing overly exciting. Just comfortable and friendly.

This we did over about a year and a half.

While we discussed marriage from time to time, and I was for it, and so was she, there was one significant hurdle. She had two twin pre-teen boys whose needs far and away superseded any other priority – like me (which I fully understood). And in that, she was a single mom, in the end, the thought of connecting with a non-Latino boy like myself for the long haul, it was too much for her to overcome.

Passing on her Hispanic culture to her almost-teen sons was of utmost importance. And the last I looked in the mirror, I was about as Caucasian as they came; white as a freshly Tide-soaked, bleached cotton tee shirt.

Plus, not to mention that I was raised in a culture way different than hers. While not an insurmountable obstacle, nevertheless, one which would require enormous give and take on both our parts.

As is common in many romantic interludes of this kind, where north meets south, eventually we moved on from one another and ventured down our separate paths. Yet, during those short eighteen months, she filled me up to the brim.

You see, Sobella was a December birthday girl.

And even if you, like me, put little stock into astrology, I knew enough that those born under the Sagittarius sign can be characterized as energetic, passionate, but above all, fun to be around.

She was those things and more, times ten. Nothing Sobella thought, felt, or did; she did halfway. It was something I truly admired. And something at this point in my life I needed to learn to embrace within myself.

People often perceive comedians to be annoyingly sanguine and impulsive, but more times than not, it is just the reverse in our day-to-day lives. Intentionally we save the ever-silly Jerry Lewis nuttiness routine to share with audiences when on stage.

Just being in her presence I could feel the self-inflicted chains that so seemed to strangle me for much of my adult life gradually melt away. So, too did my entrenched ever-somber melancholy. She made me feel like I could swing through the air like a circus trapeze artist, reaching higher and higher with each passing loop.

Now, don't get me wrong.

When we were together, we never did anything illegal. We'd just let loose from time to time, much like giddy sophomore college students might, to expend built-up steam from the pressures of assignment deadlines, mid-terms, and finals. Only our issues were real life, like making ends meet and securing a future – things that truly mattered.

Being in her company sure was addictive.

One night, I remember quite fondly.

We drove all over the LA interstate system, from one end to another, east to west, north to south, until like four in the morning, listening to an oldies station playing on the radio, as we'd sing along to all the familiar tunes. Our windows were down, being sure to take in the wonderful fragrance of salty air from nearby cool ocean breezes.

Since arriving in America, Sobella, my junior by some years, could not resist that rock 'n roll music. Of course, neither could I. I grew up embracing those melodies, caught up with the harmonies like that of *The Four Seasons, Beach Boys, Beatles, Buckinghams,* and the *Turtles* – groups whose songs, by the words alone, made one believe anything was possible. That life ahead had promise.

How different is this today, sadly, due mainly to a cancel culture dead set on forfeiting its roots and spiritual foundation. Remove these, and all the joy of life gets taken away, too.

Nevertheless, some twenty years ago, when in the company of Sobella, and on that night, anyway, I was having the time of my life. We shot up and down the 405, then onto the 5, before crisscrossing the 101 until we'd exit to grab takeout at some open-all-night taco stand. Once our bellies were full, we'd fill up the gas tank and be off again to the midnight races, retracing our steps nearly verbatim as on the first lap only this time until dawn.

In her presence, I felt zestful and liberated – a sensation that pops into my psyche almost weekly. It is a feeling I deeply yearn again for, as I'm sure do many of you.

How in contrast is it from what we see from the Woke. They seem bent only on seeking to batten down the hatches on anything remotely fun or fits with their incomprehensible agenda.

But back to my story.

There was this other time I remember that was particularly exuberant. I had taken a day off work so we could be together. It was an October mid-morning. Only this time we found ourselves driving westward down Hollywood Boulevard.

We were stopped at a red light, waiting patiently for the light to change. When it switched to green, it was at that precise second that Sobella suddenly decided we should do our version of the once famous Chinese Fire Drill, her stepping out of the car to take over as driver, and then me getting out on my side and run over to the passenger side to ride shotgun. Of course, this irritated to no end all the self-absorbed SoCal horn-honking drivers behind us, making our charade just that more enjoyable.

After a bit more daytime cruising on the Sunset Strip, we decided to head to the *Hollywood and Highland Ovation* outdoor shopping center and do a little window peeking-in of our own.

Sobella had just driven up to the light on Highland, where you could take a left into the underground pavilion parking garage next door. But rather than shoot down the right side to pick up our ticket (like you're supposed to do), she suddenly veered left, taking us instead down the garage exit ramp.

Thank goodness it was the middle of the week, a school day, and at a time seasonally when very few tourists were in sight. This meant our chance of coming face to face with an oncoming vehicle heading out was remote at best.

We soon found a parking space, walked back up a floor or two to where the ticket station was, collected our ticket, then went back and placed it inside the car's dashboard, showing that we had indeed purchased our admissions fare for the day, should security come around and check.

Next up on the agenda was to spend a few hours browsing through the 70-plus shops. Downing a quick Mimosa to quench our thirsts, we proceeded to head back to the car where we, this time around, exited the garage the same way we entered, the correct way this time.

I was happy with the notion and suspected few, if anyone else, had the inkling to try the same feat as did we that day, at least those who were sober enough and might recall.

No harm done, yet a tad risky, sure, I admit. But with a garage speed limit of 10 mph, what likelihood was there of banging into another vehicle? Yet something inside my brain couldn't square what my too-tied-up-in-knots conscience felt as I could hear a little echo inside my head giving me a good scolding – the role the Woke is more than happy to play for us these days.

On the other hand, Sobella did not allow that voice to dominate her existence. She thought of herself as noble, having a sense of her place in the world and her relationship and right standing with the God and Father of the universe.

She was truly *fearless*, with no discredit to Taylor Swift.

Yet it was something else, more powerful, which, to this day, about her, meant even more.

It was a typical Saturday, only this time Sobella had secured an overnight babysitter earlier in the day for her boys, giving us some extra free time that night to travel back to my place in Palm Springs. Once there, we shared a half-bottle of wine; the patio sliding glass door opened wide to allow the soothing, calm desert night air to fill our lungs as we sat together on the sofa, shoes off, chatting away.

It was not uncommon on occasion for us to do this. We'd converse about this or that; before we knew it, we'd be talking philosophically about some subject one of us brought up.

That night, the topic turned to love and how best to define it. I asked Sobella, *"How does one know they're in love?"* Her response, to this day, I will never forget. Not even needing to think about it, as if she had decided the matter years back, she said, *Love is when you find yourself missing someone."*

Wow, I thought.

Could it be any more straightforward? Even the most astute Ph.D. dissertation couldn't have reached a more striking and succinct conclusion.

One experiences love most fully when they are no longer in the presence of the one(s) most cared about. – a deep, often troubling sensation of loss. A yearning felt deep inside, which makes both the heart and mind work in unison to find a way to reconnect. And often, regardless of the cost or personal risk in doing so.

It is much like the longing for eternity among those who profess to be Christians. They can hardly wait for that day when they will connect face-to-face to the Lord who gave them life and promised to deliver them heavenly salvation. It is this that motivates their every action or should be. And should propel one to live with a sense of abandonment and excitement.

As the Woke continues to tear away at the fabric of our culture, many of us are experiencing that same sense of anguish today. It is a feeling that hurts deep within our souls, as we watch the things we've come to cherish about living in "the land of the free" getting stripped and tossed aside like they are just old photographs that no longer hold value.

Regarding Sobella and I, it was not until my relationship with her ended that those eight words of her reverberated throughout my mind, much like a California tremor rattles the land and those who occupy it.

I missed her terribly. And the thing is, I still miss her ... just as I do Annie and Julieta, the other woman I dated and cared deeply about from northern Mexico.

I don't see ever *getting over them*. Nor do I want to.

Each of their faces is planted in the back of my mind like a Polaroid snapshot scanned and placed on my Google Drive with the ability to retrieve from my phone at a moment's notice.

Have I moved on from all three? Sure, but that takes nothing away from what each person meant to me. Do I have remembrances of them sketched out somewhere on my body so I can retrace those magical moments together? No, and why would I? Each person is more to me than some insignia, a stripe, or a badge of honor won in battle.

Each are human beings, as alive to me now as the day each first entered my life. Not only that, but all three changed me for the better. Forever. Because of this, I don't want them represented on my body, on a fixed surface, immovable and unchangeable, except when I might move a muscle or two doing whatever. I want them, no I *need* them affixed on my heart where the thought of them breathes eternally.

I can take comfort in this thought for it is a promise founded upon the Scriptures knowing God orchestrates all experiences to draw us to Himself. And if we allow it, these become His way of taking our eyes off ourselves, and onto what truly matters: that of responding to the needs of our fellow human Earth travelers. And to live a life that is rich, holy, and full along the way.

I'm reminded of what the church reformers wrote some 400 years ago when they created the Westminster Short Catechism, a phrase for the ages based on the book of Ecclesiastes: *What is the chief end of man? To glorify God and enjoy Him forever.*

Why is it that cancel culture fails to see that we are meant for God in as much as God for us? And that the many godly pleasures He has provided us with are there for us to relish in and give Him the praise.

I prefer to get my kicks by living life unfettered, with little apology. It's a lesson a girl from Costa Rica once taught me. Still, it's one of the hardest life lessons to learn. Shame blocks us from experiencing it at almost every turn. Is it any wonder why cancel culture would prefer us to tattoo-up rather than dare to live life spontaneously?

It is why laughter is so critical to the existence of the human spirit. God uses its ingredients of grace and mercy to free us from the shackles we so willingly allow others to place upon us.

How I proceed may not be as bold as what Sobella would do, choosing to drive down the left side in a busy Hollywood parking garage, but I'm out there, my eyes wide open, looking for what next may come my way.

It's why, I guess, amusement parks keep offering up new and ever-more thrilling rollercoasters. And why we can't resist riding them. So that we may have the chance to feel the adrenaline rush, that moment when our hearts seem to pop out of our chests, all the while as our faces turn beet red.

Coaster rides at Six Flags are there to remind everyone how life *should* be lived. It's how God intends it to be – relishing every moment of every day with the ones we love. Places and times where we get so caught up in the moment that nothing else matters. And where not one tattoo to remember it all by is even needed. Ever.

Just Keep Laughing

Once
I asked
this high school junior,
"What part of United States history"
"did he most enjoy studying?"
"Before or after the civil war?"
After giving me a strange look,
he asked,
"What's that?"
"You mean 'civil'?"
I said,
thinking I needed to clarify myself.
"No,"
he goes.
"The United States?"

While
I may be the only one left
on planet Earth
not
sporting a tattoo,
I still have one role to fill.
One of us

must be the white space
in this
huge
coast-to-coast
American-made
Ink Blot.

Is it any surprise
our police
don't want to go to work?
But there is a solution:
make it
so the criminals
don't want to go
to work
either.

My niece once asked me,
"Uncle Winnie,"
"How come you sometimes chew
"with your mouth open?"
"That's not me doing it,"
I told her.
"It's my dentures."
"Come three o'clock;"
"they switch to automatic pilot."

Finally ...
I can concentrate
on something
other than
a woman's two breasts.
It's what happens to men my age.
We sprout
two
of our own.

The IRS
tells me
I owe
them
an additional 4,000 dollars.
They claim
my jokes
aren't funny enough.
"Oh, yeah,"
I said to them,
"Well, neither are yours."

If
King Solomon,
was the wisest man

to ever live,
then what in the world
was he doing with 700 wives?
When I was married,
I counted myself
lucky each day
when I could please
one.

When twin girls
look together
at the same time
into their
bathroom mirror,
how can they be sure
they're not really
quadruplets?

Sure,
I think of committing suicide.
What stops me?
I can never decide
how I should sign the note.
Here's what
I've got so far:
"Best wishes to all."

Wynn's Window to the World

One cannot help but miss the things and people we care about. It's human.

Unfortunately, until Christ's return, dealing with loss and grief remains our lot. Only in heaven will we find release from this exhaustive state.

To your getting tattoos or adding to those you may already have, give thought to the real reason why. It may change your mind.

As to the direction cancel culture wants us all to head, I refuse to allow the Woke to remove what I know is good from my life. Or to place onto my path anything that is not beneficial to my daily spiritual renewal. Neither should you.

That pining and hunger for what is good; it exists to propel us to do what we can to hold onto those things we deeply love and care about, knowing they are good for our souls. Countering cancel culture can no longer be an option; otherwise, all that we've come to love about being an American will erode before our eyes.

Sobella taught me what an authentic life looks like and how to approach living that life to the max.

Oh, and in case you're wondering, she wore no tattoos.

... Making my advice straightforward: Consider ditching the inked-on-skin illuminations. Instead, turn your life into one mammoth, long-living, breathing masterpiece of its own.

One created by the very best of artists anywhere in the world.

You.

Chapter Eight

By Any Other Name a Smith

March, one, two, three ...

The answer. 16,397 and counting.

The question?

How many Starbucks are there currently operating within the United States?

No matter how you blend it, that's a whole heckuva lot of Joe.

It all makes me wonder, beyond coffee grinds, what else are those Seattleites swirling into all those cappuccinos, given how many of us yearn to quench our thirst with a steamy morning ration of their addicted brew.

Like clockwork, at 7:30 a.m. the drive-thru line at my neighborhood green and white edifice must have fifteen cars stacked up all in a row like obedient army ants – the drivers loyal to the death, waiting patiently at the window, ready to collect their java fixes and marching orders for the day.

More than in any other nation, I suspect, consumers in America are adept at getting on the bandwagon of the latest trends, be it in clothes, music, or whatever. And once hooked, staying loyal to the cause. Regardless of the cost.

Cancel culture, fully aware of this phenomenon, takes full advantage. The Woke are masters at disseminating their propaganda, hopeful that whatever the newest item on their agenda can remain in the news cycle long enough, most in society will, without question, dance along to the music and, like Starbucks loyalists, soon enough, fall in line.

Only with the Woke, it's not a cup of coffee they're peddling – it's more. Way more.

A Telling Tale

I'm not a sadist. I'm not.

It's just that I love playing pranks on people. It's the nature, I guess of most comedians.

Even as a little kid, I found ways to surprise and tease my grandparents. If the jokes were harmless enough, my parents didn't seem to mind much.

When I became an adult, not much changed.

Once, for April Fools, when I was director of public relations and donor development at a distinguished university on the outskirts of Chicago, I left notes in the mailbox for half my staff, telling them their services were no longer required. I convinced the other half they needed to turn in their comfy school-furnished Toyota Camrys, and, in place, each would be given keys to the worst car ever made – a Yugo.

Tricks are great if done in fun.

And just so you know, an hour later, after pulling that hoax on my staff, I reminded them it was April 1st – which everybody then sighed in relief.

Playing practical jokes on close friends is incredibly gratifying and part-devilish, especially when the person you're playing it on never sees it coming. Or better still, they can't ever figure out who's the culprit behind the charade.

I equate it to standing three feet above a laboratory maze where you, like an NFL team owner, tucked inside your warm, *Hors d' oeuvres* furnished skybox, watch the bemused mice below to see how quickly – before time runs out – make it from one end of the labyrinth to the other, their tiny noses twitching frantically as they catch the scent of distant cheese propelling them onward.

This was me one day during my senior year in college when my room-mate and I, working as the mad lab scientists, initiated a game of cat and mouse on a friend who also resided in the same dorm; we the curious cats, our friend, the befuddled mouse.

I was a student at a small midwestern, prestigious university known for its strong academic reputation. The school, even back then, being quite tuned into the importance of avoiding exclusivity, though never making a big deal about it, had a policy that did not permit campus fraternities or sororities of any kind.

Save one, an honor's dorm solely for men, a tradition dating back many years before I arrived on the scene.

Even writing about it now, I'm sure it was the university's way to lasso the ever-bored rambunctious intellectual types all under one roof, thereby knowing should the collective smarts of young adult boys fire up some crafty, crazy scheme, as in *Animal House*, all property damage would be contained to the oldest building on campus.

The same dorm building exists today, with the aid of a capital cam-paign to refurbish the structure, which now serves to house a few of the school's administrative offices. When I first arrived as a freshman, the over-50-year-old brick property was most assuredly on the downslope.

After each summer recess, I'd half expected to return to campus only to find it demolished. The place was that ancient, still safely habitable, but barely.

The dorm was a small, rectangular structure with three floors and a basement. The cellar was used as the men's TV lounge and game area. On each floor were two wings, one to the left, one to the right, just four rooms to each wing, where the rooms housed only two persons – a total of just forty-eight men altogether.

I remember room ceilings being exceptionally high, as was the custom in the early 20th century to make them – practically over 11 feet tall. Complementary in each room were creaky wood floors, and two oversized windows with a white-painted steam radiator that sat underneath. What an awful noise these made each time water would work its way up through the cylinders.

Connecting the wings on each floor was an exceedingly long stairwell, a Victorian-style switchback staircase: Eight switchbacks in all when you counted from the bottom where the basement began. Each grouping of steps was extra wide, so much so that one year, rumor had it that some of the "gentlemen" discussed trying to see if they might manage to commandeer a big rig cab, its engine removed, no doubt, and push it somehow up to the top floor.

Now, as to the length of each staircase, a single runway incorporated a good nearly 25 steps, a stupendous expanse. The first time I ever found myself inside the dorm, I came to visit a friend who resided there. I was captivated when I needed to climb the stairs to the 3rd floor, where his room was stationed.

Doing so, it was easy to envision myself as Rhett Butler in *Gone with the Wind*, carrying Scarlett upstairs where soon I'd make passionate love to her, but only after first needing to regain my strength by resting a half-day or more to catch my breath.

Because the building was so old, unlike other dorms on campus being more modern and up to date, and which hosted a multitude of phones on every floor, campus operations put in only two central phone lines in this small dorm: a single customary campus extension phone way up on the third floor and the second floor, one pay phone (pre-cell phone days) booth and all. Both were situated in the brief passageway connecting each wing, a few feet from the staircase.

Even with these disadvantages, something was incredibly alluring to both male and female students about the place. Strolling past the dorm to classes each week during my first two years, I recall always wishing I might someday be one of the select few forty-eight students chosen for the inside. Somehow, it fitted the self-image I created for myself.

Egotistical, I know, but confession is good for the soul.

Yet I knew my GPA would never be high enough, and it would take me getting accepted into graduate school when I finally realized the secret to obtaining good grades – working extra hard. A prerequisite to achieving anything in life that is worthwhile. And a concept, by the way, the Woke seems resistant to embrace.

Plus, I reasoned, what chance did I genuinely have of being accepted? When vacancies seldom did occur, students would rush to apply, like when hoping to be first in line at the Apple store on Black Friday to collect the latest model iPhone.

But what the heck, I said to myself. What did I have to lose?

So, when an opening popped up near the end of my junior year, I submitted my lowly credentials. To my utter surprise, I made the first cut. Next would be individual interviews, group interviews, and other admit proceedings. Somehow, I managed to get through each, enduring them all.

Long story short, I made it in.

How I did so, even to this day, I have little clue.

An intellectual, I was not. And still not. Intuitive, yes, but book smart, no way. My grades were decent but never something you'd write home about. I think what clinched it was that repeatedly, I kept telling the guys during the interviews that I would contribute positively to the history and legacy of the place.

And by the time I graduated, you could say I had. At least in one way.

My reputation on this mostly everybody-knows-everybody-else, 1,600-student campus was I was more than friendly and always one to volunteer for tasks most others seldom wanted to take on. Something that always wins bonus points. I was also known for something else – one who, on occasion, could come up and deliver some of the most extraordinary campus-wide escapades of all time.

Like when I played a beauty on one of our Business Department's dearly loved professors. It was his wedding anniversary the next day, and for weeks previously in class, he kept lamenting how, if only he and his wife could get away, even if for a few short days, and visit Hawaii. The never-ending winter Midwest days of clouds and below-freezing temperatures could play havoc with your head.

After stewing on it for a bit, I devised a way to make it *seem* like he had. Only how to go about putting my master plan into effect was the question.

What I had conjured up would require me to somehow get past campus security and gain access to the instructor's office after midnight – which I succeeded at, though I cannot recall precisely how I managed to pull it off without getting caught.

Nevertheless, the sequence's next steps were a breeze once in. With my props pre-loaded earlier in the day onto a large platform dolly, I quickly turned his office into a makeshift tropical beach paradise. Complete with three inches of white sand stretched out on the floor, two seven-foot-tall palm trees, a hammock reaching between the two, a couple of coconuts for good measure, Hawaiian lei strung about, and luau music synchronized to play the second he'd open his door first thing the following morning.

If nothing more than by a matter of elimination, everyone surmised it was the work of Wynn Holly.

Of course, later that day, the professor invited his wife to stop by and take in the scene before the janitorial staff returned the room to its original, faculty-office bland appearance, complete with scattered papers and files spread everywhere.

Again, just like when I was a child, the caper I pulled off that night was relatively harmless, as such stunts should always be. Oh, and yes, I did help the custodians with clearing out the room after, as that was only right to do.

So, as you can see, only in part did I figure my getting into the honor dorm came from my pure academic qualifications; my suspicion was, even to this day, it had more to do with my reputation as being bright in another sense, that of being clever, savvy, and a bit rogue.

But back to the game of cat and mouse.

It was a usual late October Saturday in the dorm, and in between studying, guys would hang out in the basement lounge and absorb themselves in whatever Big 10 football matchup was on the tube. One of the students watching was a senior with the last name of Smyth. Sam lived on the third floor, while my room was on the second. Both our rooms were positioned closest to the respective phones.

On weekends when either of the two hallway central phones would ring, the informal rule was that whoever was around and nearest to the phone picked it up. Then it would be this person's job to knock on the door of the person asked for, but if gone, to take down a message and tape it on their door.

On Saturdays and Sundays, several long-distance calls came in from family members, most often to the pay phone on my floor. As my room was just a few steps away from the phone, retrieving calls often fell to me. Not that I minded it all that much.

My routine always was to schedule a study session on Saturday afternoons, leaving the evening for relaxation or a date (when I was lucky enough to summon one). So when the pay phone would ring, it was customary that I'd respond to Ma Bell and leave the room and answer her call. Even answering the phone on the third floor, the other guys soon enough came to assume I'd respond to that one, too. New kid on the block, I guess.

Well, as you can imagine, not only did all of this, over time, become a nuisance, but it also soon tended to interrupt my thought process to the point that on some autumn Saturdays, I never felt I was accomplishing anything.

Finally, on this particular afternoon, I had reached my limit.

My roommate Kevin was studying with me at his desk, and he had about had it, too. What with all the incoming phone calls we started to feel like we were a two-member relay team competing in an Olympic medley race – the phone's receivers serving as the batons.

Midterms were around the corner, and being one of the more academically challenged students in the dorm, I needed to hold onto any extra study prep time I could get. Only I wasn't succeeding, not in the least.

Often to avoid having to be the designated message secretary for the day, guys would park themselves in the basement until way past dark, never once coming out to see the light of day. On this football sport-filled afternoon, Mr. Smyth mirrored this to a tee.

This caused Kevin and I to decide it was high time to cook up a plan to alter the landscape, making our first target Sam.

In this case, to force Sam off his butt and make him deal with what he seemed unwilling to pitch in and do.

Sam was a friend, mind you, a good one, but friendship has limitations.

Since our school was a small campus, we all had easy access to the student directory – a hard copy back then. It showed that there were two other male students listed with the same-sounding last name as our dearest dorm companion Sam. Both were pronounced the same way, though each was spelled differently; a *Smith* (the most common spelling) and a *Smieth*.

One resided in a large, all-male dorm on the other side of the Quad, while the second lived off-campus in an apartment yet nearby. Of course, what made the upcoming prank even more satisfying to divvy out was our knowledge that all three males were acquainted with one another and how often it was that people got the three of them mixed up.

Two of them were majoring in the same field even, engineering, which added to our fun.

So, with the foundation laid, Kevin and I put our collected, devious minds to work.

Act I

The main storyline required us to pretend to call into the dorm from "somewhere else," still using one of the two phones already in the dorm to place the unexpected call. Using the third-floor phone, we'd dial the number to the second dorm phone, the pay phone, and then be sure to ask to speak to Sam Smyth. Immediately, I would answer and head to the basement, retrieve Sam, and then wait and see what would happen next.

Kevin got the whole ball rolling by making the first call, using the 3rd-floor campus extension phone, and dialing the pay phone number on the floor below. Of course, as previously arranged, I picked it up.

"Hello ... just a minute. I'll get him."

Next, I rushed down to the basement, pretending to act flustered; I told *our* Mr. Smyth he had an important call waiting for him upstairs on the pay phone.

An incoming call on the pay phone was believed to be nine times out of ten from a family member, usually mom or dad, and as a result, most always prompted an immediate response from the recipient, the son, in this case, our Sam.

As it would happen, and right on cue, Sam shot up the three flights of stairs to get to the phone as quickly as possible. And me, of course, following directly behind. But as soon as he started to pick up the receiver, I, standing nearby, signaled Kevin upstairs, at that precise moment, waving to him through an opening in the grand staircase, to hang up on his end.

"Hello, hello," we hear Sam say repeatedly, puzzled that no one is on the other end.

Not overthinking it, Sam placed the receiver back on the phone, then traced downstairs to the basement to enjoy the rest of the games, figuring it must've been a wrong number.

Kevin and I waited a minute or two, just enough for Sam to settle in, and we replayed the same scenario.

Only this time, though, rather than running down the stairs to collect Sam, I stayed where I was, yelling to him below, loudly mirroring the sound that a bull horn makes, hollering that he's got another call on the pay phone and he should hurry to come and answer right away.

At once, like the crack of thunder following a lightning rod shooting to Earth, all you could hear was *boom, boom, boom,* the sound of tennis shoes pounding on the steps below as Sam hurriedly skipped over every other stair to be sure to arrive at the phone before the same person (who must be waiting patiently now for a second time) once again gets frustrated and decides to hang up.

But like before, too late, as the same thing transpires.

Like great conductors leading a grand symphony orchestra, Kevin and I had our timing down to perfection. With a shake of his head and a tad out of breath, Sam saunters below to the man cave, where he had been up until now, seated comfortably in one of the oversized comfy chairs.

We let another minute or so go by. Then onto ....

Act II

This go round, however, I made it a point to position myself on the pay phone pretending to chat away, giving the impression that I was knee-deep in some all-consuming conversation. However, what I'd done, was call the upstairs 3rd-floor campus extension, whereas before we did, I asked for Mr. Smyth.

Only this time, to be sure to cover our tracks, Kevin was there waiting to pick it up. We enlisted a fellow dorm mate, making his way down to the TV room, to let Sam know he had a call waiting.

Only this time not on floor number two, but way up on floor number three ... and, once again, to *hurry!*

Sure enough, just like before, we could make out the sound of Sam flying out of his cushion Lazy Boy; this time, however, he needed to do double time to get up to the last floor, four total flights up, some 100 plus steps.

Excellent training, no doubt, for one planning to be a fireman, but way over the top for Sam, bent solely on a career as a seat-beckoned electrical design engineer.

Acutely out of breath, he picked up the phone. I, on the other end, pretending to be someone else by disguising my voice, asked for Jeffrey Smith – which our dorm resident Sam absolutely was not.

Gasping for air, Sam was forced to tell the person on the other end of the line – me – that I must've dialed the wrong number.

The call ends, leaving our main character, like a Golden Retriever puppy, having been led into playing a game of endless fetch, to descend once again the four-floor staircase down to the submarine deck 80 feet below the surface.

Little did Sam know Kevin and I weren't done playing yet, not by a long shot.

After all, we still had one more *Smyth* to fry, this time by the spelling, *S-m-i-e-t-h*. An uncommon spelling of the name yet found in certain pockets of the country.

Act III

The climax came when we enlisted the aid of two friends from a nearby dorm to pitch in and participate in our play-on-words game – a couple of fellow engineering majors of Sam's.

Our first volunteer was Sara. We had her pretend to be the school nurse. Her task was to call into the third-floor extension and ask for Mister Smyth.

The purpose of her call was to share with him some test results we knew he had been waiting to hear about from lab work taken the day before. Nothing serious, but to confirm that he did not have the early makings of strep throat and only the cold which had been spreading throughout campus the past several weeks.

Only now, by utilizing a third outside line, we could stage our plan so that two calls for Sam could come in near simultaneously, which we went on to achieve most beautifully.

Playing Nurse Betty, our female-in-arms, after some initial chit-chat, pauses a second on the line only to inform Sam that she thinks she may have mistakenly dialed up the wrong "Smith", leaving our highly winded dorm contestant more bewildered than ever.

Of course, she apologizes profusely before hanging up, making Sam wonder, at this point, what the heck is going on.

But no sooner than Sam places down the receiver, I call him to race down quick-like to the second floor to retrieve an incoming call, now on the pay phone, right below him.

Little to Sam's knowledge, the whole setup has been a ploy to run Sam ragged and in circles, and in so doing, to motivate him to change course. In particular, to decide to remain on the third floor, or at least close enough to it, and be available to field any incoming afternoon calls the remainder of the day.

As Sam hurriedly makes his way down to the second floor, our friend, Markus, portraying the school's electrical science professor Dr. Tim Johnson, is ready to fulfill his part as he waits to speak with Sam.

The reason? To review with him an assignment Sam recently turned in.

However, this setup was equally bogus. Our "professor", after ensuring Sam has taken the bait, informed him that he is sorry but now realizes he, too, like the nurse, must've gotten ahold of the wrong "Smith," And that he had meant all along to speak with the other one in the class, Brent Smieth.

At this point, our pigeon in this human pinball, shell game of ours, having jumped from phone to phone, is now way beyond exhaustion.

Yet still, given all this, Sam was determined to make his way down those many stairs one final time. But as he began, taking no more than a few steps past the second-floor staircase, he paused. Engulfing air like a blowfish, his one arm leaning on the banister for support, he finally decides best to hang up his hat and call it a day.

As he headed back to the 3rd floor, Kevin and I watched our slow-motion moving, huffing, and puffing two-legged mouse amble his way up the next flight to his room door. Once there, turning the knob, we heard him utter to himself, *"I can't believe it; I just can't believe it."*

Once safely inside, Kevin and I gave each other a high five. A victory conceived; a battle won.

Yes, language can be immensely confusing, whatever the subject in focus. When applied to entertain as with that all-time classic skit from Abbott and Costello, *Who's on First*, it is an absolute delight.

But language can also be employed to take advantage of others, to make others feel bad about themselves, and even to tear people apart.

Unlike the hoax, we played on Sam, cancel culture has been making use of language to rearrange society. What most of us know to be fact, they have worked tirelessly to twist words around so that what once was correct no longer seems true.

When the Woke tells us that a man can be a woman, or that a woman, a man, something is out of kilter. Yet how surprising it is to see many in society seem to want to go along with such nonsense.

We all have the power to follow the beat of another drum, preferably directives first laid down for us by our nation's forefathers – those mostly built upon a Judeo-Christian heritage.

Best to never allow word-play tricks or the way-over-the-top definitions the Woke gives to stuff to lead us down a path that takes us to nowhere. Listen closely to what your heart is instructing you on; it is God's gift to discern the truth.

Like the aroma of a cup from Starbucks, the call of cancel culture's siren is tempting, Yet, we need not have to respond.

When we make up our minds that their overpriced cup of Java isn't worth all the fuss, maybe then we will see things more clearly.

Just Keep Laughing

When
I first learned
to play tennis,
it was the best thing ever.
Finally,
a game
where I can
be beating
the daylights out of my opponent,
yet at the same
exact moment
be screaming
across the net,
I *love* them.

Sometimes
I forget
where I am.
Does this ever happen to you?
Yesterday,
in the grocery checkout line,
on the conveyor belt
along with the bread and milk,
I laid out

my belt, cell phone, and wallet.
Thank goodness
the cashier
was there
to stop and remind me:
"Sir, don't forget your shoes."

Why is it
each time
I head into
a Japanese Steakhouse -
I have this nagging feeling
I should've
updated my Will?
All those
flying knives and cleavers ....
It's the one restaurant
where I'm
just as glad
to be walking out
as I am
walking in.

What
if we humans
were the ones
locked behind cages at the zoo?

What might the animals who visit
say about us?
"Let's go over there"
"and see the 'Politicians'?"
says the first bear.
"What's the point?"
bemoans the second.
"All they do all day is just sit there."

Here's how
I know
if tomorrow
will turn out
cool and overcast.
The 6 o'clock weather guy
will predict
hot and sunny.

How
do I define
retirement?
Three words.
Dinner at three.

I see
Disney's
made it in the news again.
This time
to unveil
its brand-new rollercoaster:
THE CHANGER.
What a perfect name for it, too.
As you finish
a strange sensation
comes over you
that the sex
you believed you were
born as
turns out
all these years
you've been
the complete
opposite.

Wives
often complain
to me,
that the only thing
their husbands
think about
is sex.
Now,

I can't speak for other men,
but as for me
most times,
I'm hardly thinking
at all.

The last time
I was at my dentist,
I told him,
"Guess what?"
"I'm now flossing every night."
"Great,"
he responded.
"Everything's much cleaner, right?"
"Sure is,"
I told him.
"But my ass is killing me."

Wynn's Window to the World

An organization's marketing and promotion centers on calculated strategies to convince consumers to think about their product how they need it to be.

I know how it works.

I was the director of consumer research at two midwestern advertising agencies.

Just like with Starbucks, if done well, soon enough, all will buy into how the company is positioning its brand solely based on habit, precisely what their sales plan has been all along from the beginning. It's why you see more and more of those famous white and green logo stands popping up all the time and on every other corner.

Consumers can't help but surmise it must be the best coffee on the market; how else could they afford to keep building all those stores?

It's the same type of mass-marketing campaign arranged by cancel culture. Like Starbucks, the Woke has perpetrated a number on society by making inroads into the American psyche. One idea at a time.

We see it within education, politics, sports, leisure, and even, of late now, the church.

While their messaging informs us it centers on inclusion and diversity (all for the common good, they claim), the hidden truth is that few among the Woke desire unity in any way, shape, or form.

Regrettably, to the average everyday person, it's hard to distinguish fact from fiction, good from bad, or beneficial from detrimental.

And the tool the Woke likes to use the most?

Language.

They employ it to confuse the public into thinking that what we all used to believe to be false is, in fact, true.

But we needn't be fooled.

It is all sleight of hand, just an illusion.

It is a trick, not done in jest like the one Kevin and I played on our good friend Sam, but one to sway and hoodwink those upon which it is manufactured.

How often lately have we heard that inflation is no longer a bad thing; it is a "healthy transition." Or the term sexual deviation no longer needs to be used, heck, no. Instead, better if we simply label it "fluidity."

Hogwash.

Refrain, my friends, from finding yourself caught off guard. Cancel Culture desires we embrace their way of thinking and living, or not at all. And once enough become caught up in it, they figure that, it will become ever more challenging to turn back the clock.

Only that's a misnomer, as well.

Time can be moved around. It's done all the time to achieve the intended result.

In America, we do it as a country, twice a year, once in the spring, and once in the autumn, to mark the beginning and end of daylight-saving time.

Just like with Starbucks coffee, simply because it happens to be around the corner doesn't mean you or I must swing by and purchase a cup. I can say no. And so can you. LOUDLY.

The same can be said about what the Woke is trafficking.

Our chuckling at their blarney, when done in unison, cancel culture will soon discover that the last laugh will be on them.

And one which most will never see coming.

Chapter Nine

Damn, My Ass Hurts

They, them, thee and thou.

Can it be any more ego-centric than this – than to require others to call you by some made-up prefix or title?

Preferred pronouns may seem important to a few, but to most of us, no matter what Sam, Dick, or Harry they're attached to (or their respective female counterparts), the rest of us could care less.

I recall, in grammar school, even back then, having trouble distinguishing when to use the correct pronoun. Now, cancel culture wants to throw in all kinds of ridiculous options, like a multiple-choice question on an SAT test, where I'm supposed to see if I can get the answer correct on the first try.

Most days, I'm happy if I can remember my own name.

Furthermore, how people evaluate one another is rarely based on superficial titles. It is something else entirely. Is a person helpful? Do they put in a good 8-hour day at work? Do they show kindness? Is what they say consistent with their actions? Most of all, do they speak the truth?

These are the things the other 99 percent focus on. Not they, them, thee, thou, or whatever colloquial is the current flavor of the week.

Call me old-fashioned, but I want to be judged by what I do. As I indicated in a previous chapter, this alone is a hard enough task for me to live up to – not whether I'm following the rules of Woke pronouns.

People can play the name game all day, but in the end, doesn't it only exacerbate social justice divisions all that more?

The whole affair reminds me of that famous, long-standing Star-Kist Tuna TV commercial. We see Charlie hell-bent, much like a stuck-up, nose-in-the-air art connoisseur, on delivering to us land lover humans who reside above the water's surface, tuna, that has good taste. But he has to be reminded constantly by his fishy friend that the only thing that people want and care about is tuna that taste good.

The same can be applied to pronouns. The idea is interesting, I guess, but does it truly matter?

Not in the least.

A Telling Tale

Leonardo was quite the character.

And very much the handful, too, or as the Spanish might label him, *"desafios,"* meaning challenging. But what a great kid. And just shy of four years old. The fist son of Julieta.

Julieta was by far the most intriguing creature of the female variety I've ever met. Born in Mexico, she grew up on the northern border of Sonora, across the Arizona state line, just shy of Tucson, only a few short hours away.

While living in the hot southwestern desert, I met her on one of my journeys south. Soon enough, because of her, I suspect, and my growing fondness for Mexican culture, I eventually became certified in English as a Second Language so that I could take a year-long sabbatical from my college duties and transplant myself there to teach.

I served as a visiting adjunct professor at a branch campus of a well-respected Guadalajara university. In addition, I taught in a K-12 school, instructed Mexican-born corporate executives in American business and marketing management practices, and on weekends, in my "spare" time, ran a small ESL workshop for young adults in my all-cinder block, typical no-heat home in the local barrio where I resided.

I've always felt that if one wants to immerse oneself in another country's culture or venture on some Johnny-be-do-Gooder mission trip, one needs to become like the people who live there, meaning *you do what they do* and *take on the challenges of everyday life they face.* Which for me frequently meant not having hot water, having my electric power cut off more than just a little, needing to walk most places, or if the spirit prompted me to hop on an overcrowded half-working city bus to get around, risking life and limb.

In other words, by choice, I was incredibly inconvenienced every day. Still, it proved to be an experience I found rewarding and meaningful on every level. It was a time when I knew my faith in God would either get stronger or fall off a cliff. For me, it was the former.

As to Julieta, sometimes spelled *Yulieta* in Spanish, where the J is left off in pronunciation and given more of a "ya" sound, my getting to know and being around her was unmatched by any experience I had with a woman up to that time, or since.

Leonardo was so much like her.

Bold, even to the point of being brazen at times, yet also spontaneously sensitive and sweet, which made spying on him from a distance feel like I was doing reconnaissance surveillance, playing the role of secret agent 007 which I found a bit devious but delightful. It was like that marvelous sensation when treated unexpectedly to some beautiful scenery of nature, like a sweeping landscape of lush purple wildflowers spilling out for miles and miles across an enchanted meadow.

I took to Leonardo almost as much as I did Julieta. And he took to me.

One memory of him rises to my consciousness almost weekly – my holding him in my lap, one Saturday at the movie theatre, the two of us together, accompanied by Julieta, watching the latest Pixar flick, which suddenly he has lost interest in. Due mainly, I'm sure, to his having gobbled down in less than 25 minutes flat, a giant-size order of nachos, one strawberry crepe, a mini corndog on a stick, and an ever-so-sweet, Mexican-brewed Horchata.

His stomach was full, making him beyond content. So, he did what any child at that age would do next. He fell asleep in the arms of anyone possessing him.

In this case, his male playmate companion and adult protector, me.

As for Julieta, ours was a spring-autumn affair, like the kind often pictured in one of those romantic 1950s black-and-white big-screen classics; I played the much older man, and Julieta, the much younger woman. Though frowned upon here in the States, this scenario is observed more often than one might think in less advanced countries, with very little fanfare or something considered nefarious.

Despite our age separations, Julieta and I were more than Sympatico, closer to identical twins who could read each other's minds and say what the other one was thinking, even before they said it. We shared many of the same values, a remarkably similar sense of humor, and nearly indistinguishable perspectives on life.

All who knew us saw us as a good match.

When out on a date at a restaurant, we'd often liked to play a game that we labeled *Pregunta,* simply meaning "Question." We'd take turns asking one another about our likes and dislikes, sometimes speaking English, sometimes Spanish. It became our way to learn about each other's minds, hearts, and souls.

Now, on this early autumn weekend trip to what seemed like my second home (this being a year or so before I decided to teach in Mexico), I learned Leonardo had developed a nasty case of diarrhea. And that it had been going on for nearly three days straight. No real fever to speak of, just an untimely case of the constant runs.

As to the cause, no one could say.

But most likely, it resulted from him having downed some lousy unfiltered water, the main ingredient used to make a *Raspado,* a fruity ice-like slushy drink, a standard beverage and treat in Mexico that kids ... and adults love. Montezuma's Revenge affects not just tourists but all who reside throughout Mexico. Only in places like the US is access to clean water taken for granted. It remains a constant worry and threat in developing countries and the third world.

With the number of visits Leonardo had made to the bathroom during the week, Julieta had lost count by this time. The total, nevertheless, remained high and most certainly tallied way in the upper double digits. While I was there, you could almost set your clock by when he would need to high-tail it down the narrow hall to the bathroom, hoping he'd get there in the nick of time.

I felt for the kid.

It's hard enough for an adult to mess with such annoyances, but for a youngster, I'm sure he must've wondered if this real-life nightmare would ever end. It did, of course, but not for a few more days.

At least it had yet to reach its conclusion as of Sunday morning, the final day of my weekend visit, before returning to Tucson for another work week. Though we saw signs of improvement, the harmful microorganism playing havoc with his intestines was determined not to go down without swinging.

Still, we chose to try our best to make it to church this morning anyway. Only, we decided we'd better sit in the back pew, just in case we all had to make a quick getaway for reasons not apparent to the casual observer.

Julieta's mother and stepfather, her *tia* and *tio* (aunt and uncle), and a few of Leonardo's cousins had planned to join us. In Spanish culture, any event becomes a multi-family affair. All had arrived at the house and waited patiently in the living room for Leonardo to conclude his final pit stop before we left home.

When we were about to exit the front door, Leonardo felt it best to bring everyone up to speed about his predicament, just so that we all had a realistic expectation on how things could go over the next few hours.

He placed his right-hand flank around his left waist to meet his left buttock, then gently patted it as if to say, *please, please, for once, give me a break.*

Then looking up to the heavens, as if appealing to God, he shook his little boy head, and as he did, uttered, *"Damn, my ass hurts."*

We all burst into laughter.

How could we not?

The very fact that at his tender age, he could not only identify the direct source of his aggravation but, just like an adult might, speak to the suffering forthwith, so familiar to our human condition, almost as if he was C. S. Lewis himself, the world renown, now deceased Christian writer and apologist, declaring it.

The entire two-minute scene was pure amusement.

More than this, though, he spoke the truth. His rear end felt sore because it was sore.

Had he or Julieta been able to determine the exact cause of the infraction, whatever juice flavor may have triggered the torment these past five days, she would have seen to it that he never ordered that concoction again.

Unlike in the US where there are rigorous inspections and quality control requirements for the manufacturing of food and drinks, in Mexico, while structures are in place, these are in no way consistently monitored. There simply lacks the resources or manpower. So, should a company, from time to time, feel a need to shade off some corners of the process, or refrain from sound product measurement procedures, here or there, to mount a tad more profit, oh well.

Yet someone in the public does pay for it. And in this scenario, that someone was little Leonardo.

Unfortunately, the likes of cancel culture can be described in much the same way. Society is getting ill from their preposterous notions.

Like a few unscrupulous overlooked companies in a developing country, they remain laser-focused on manufacturing their propaganda, minimizing the needs and wants of all else, regardless of how anyone else may feel about the matter.

And, just like in Leonardo's case, it has become a royal pain in the butt for the rest of us. Even to the point where some are losing their jobs or are being denied promotions over not abiding by their made-up, non-commissioned rules.

Like in not addressing others by using the proper pronoun etiquette.

It's beyond time to call it what it is:

Gibberish gobbledygook.

Just Keep Laughing

My tattoo artist
tells me
next week
he's planning
this great
two-for-one sale.
Get the first two tattoos
at the regular amount of pain,
and the third one,
he'll do it
at half
the pain off.

From
now on,
here's my feeling
about diseases.
If we can't
pronounce or spell it,
we shouldn't be allowed to get it.

And
another thing.
Should
Dr. Fauci
ever again
tell all of us
to do something ...
Here's what I'm planning to do:
the absolute
opposite.

My dentist
told me
my dentures needed braces.
"Oh, come on,"
I said to him.
Oh, no Wynn, it's true,"
he replied.
"But not to worry,"
he added.
"Unlike at fifteen,"
"when you first had them put on,"
"this time,"
"they'll never hurt a bit."

The only difference
between those
who believe in God
from those who don't -
What life insurance coverage
you qualify for.
The Christian:
Whole Life.
The atheist:
Term only.

Tell me
if I'm wrong,
but
when two people
at the same time
play solitaire -
isn't that like cheating?

In Palm Springs,
California,
a predominantly gay community
where I once lived -
each morning for exercise
I liked walking
past the local Dog Park.
Only I never could believe

the number
I saw in heat.
... As for the dogs -
they just liked
fetching tennis balls.

To
control inflation,
economists
tell us
we all need
to be
doing more of one thing:
spending less
than we make.
For crying out loud,
who in the world
wants to do that?

Yesterday
near the mall
I happened by
this brand-new
vape shop.
All

who entered
got greeted
by their sign -
CAUTION:
LOW VISIBILITY AHEAD.

My dermatologist told me
never to scratch
when I get an itch.
That's like having a bowl of M&M's
sitting a top of your coffee table
and being told,
"Just count them."

I'm
beginning
to think
God
must have it in for me.
My underwear
just filed for divorce.
Irreconcilable small differences.

I
make it a point
each day,
to read a little fiction.
It helps
take my mind off food.
If only now
I could teach
my stomach
to read.

I just added
a new routine
to my stand-up act.
A ventriloquist bit.
My doll is
Joy Behar
from *The View*.
At first,
it worked out great.
She talked, then I spoke.
But now ...
seven weeks in -
I can't get the dummy to shut up.

Wynn's Window to the World

You can't help but wonder, what is the pronoun craze truly about?

My sense is it all boils down to one thing: a need we all feel to belong to something bigger than ourselves – the deepest, I suspect, of all human longings.

So, in that sense, I can't fault those knee-deep in cancel culture for wanting to use them.

Yet here is the thing. The more the focus is on how people want to be labeled, the less room there is left over to recognize the virtues (and needs) we all possess within.

My suggestion to the Woke is this.

Be you he, she, they, or it – drop the narcissism routine. Instead, work on listening and attending to the real needs of others around you. While I might be off base here, I tend to feel it's the best way to get others to notice you.

Then, as for the rest of us in the non-woke camp, the next time you do a wash, do what I'm thinking about doing. While it will be a tight fit, I plan to toss myself into the machine instead of sticking my clothes in. All that spinning around and percolating is bound to do a world of good.

Not only will it help to soften me around the edges, but it's likely to straighten out all the erroneous thinking cancel culture has inundated us with over these past several years.

Consider it like baptism.

Oh, and finally, in case the Woke cares to know what are the preferred pronouns I go by – two words:

Bite me.

Chapter Ten

"Newspaper!"

But my horoscope said it was supposed to be a good day.

The problem with taking a horoscope at face value is that you never really know if what is predicted will come true as you start out your day.

And should you go too overboard in believing what is written, you can easily find yourself acting in such a way by bringing what is on paper into existence – which is precisely the whole hidden point behind most authors who write them.

More times than not, however, if you're like me ... maybe only a fraction of what I see forecasted ever comes to fruition. It's often just the reverse; it's way off.

It could be said the same, too, about psychics and their stream-of-consciousness prophesies. Not to dismiss clairvoyant people (I've known a few, and believe me, these folks are genuinely gifted), but most life forecasters are, at best, mere sleight-of-hand artists or, at worst, pure charlatans.

Yet this is precisely how those in cancel culture want you to take note of their prognostications; that they have been chosen, assigned by the universe to be society's fortune tellers. They spin their tale, doing so with unparalleled determination, making sure we buy into all their misconstrued reality. The likes that not even David Copperfield, by his remarkable wizardly ways, could conjure up.

Acting like writers of a tabloid horoscope, the Woke has convinced many right-minded skeptics that should they even utter the slightest thought of not "believing" in their folly, this should be taken as an unadulterated sin. And consequently, those unrepentant nonbelievers should be ostracized and exiled for openly defying cancel culture's mandate to play by the new rule order.

All nonbelievers, they claim, are either ignorant, non-feeling, or downright insensitive toward the human condition. One must mirror how the Woke thinks and sees things; otherwise, don't bother to leave the house.

If this scenario were being written about, and thereby confined solely within the world of literature, it would be well to classify this story as a tragedy.

Call me sentimental, but I like it when the story ends well.

... For everyone concerned.

A Telling Tale

You couldn't get around him.

I'm telling you; you just couldn't. And it wasn't that the guy was that big. Still, he scared the bejeebers out of you. All of us in the neighborhood knew his reputation and did everything possible to stay clear of Courtney whenever we could.

But for Annie and I, we were stuck.

Courtney lived right below us, occupying, with his dad, Randolph, the first floor of a huge old southwestern Virginia, Victorian house. Randolph was the owner.

On the second floor, he divided the large upstairs into two apartments, each grand in scale. We were lucky enough to have rented out the largest unit. It would be our first home together as husband and wife.

Living there reminded me of what it must've felt like before the Civil War when large southern plantation dwellers ruled the roost. It was a time when each mansion and its adjacent spread glistened the wooded landscape. And where the savory scent of something cooking could be seen rising from the kitchen chimney, beckoning those outside the four walls tending the crops or hunting, to come home for a hearty meal.

Our unit alone, on its own merits, was incredible.

Pane class doors served as the entryway to every room. Large, almost Jeffersonian *Monticello*-like windows peered over the manicured garden below. Thin original pine floorboards squeaked at the mere sense of stocking feet about to step on one of its stain-varnished planks.

Down the hall from the two oversized bedrooms was a high-ceiling dining room, and next to it was an old linoleum-floor kitchen, complete with traditional, white-painted cabinetry. Near the front of the apartment was a small but eloquent-squared living room, the outside wall supporting an all-brick fireplace and mantle, a window on either side of it. To the right side of the room was another class-paned door that led out to an enormous, covered porch balcony.

During the summer months, we'd sit out there at night and catch the thunderous rainstorms blowing in, giving much relief to those hot Blue Ridge Mountain muggy days.

Mostly it was a very pleasant start to our new life together. Or at least those first few weeks could have been had it not been for you know who.

Almost like clockwork, at the end of every workday, as Annie and I would drive home and park our shared lone, one car on the street below, we'd see Courtney out front, a look of intention as if he had invested his entire morning and afternoon to plan his attack.

We'd be forced into taking a deep breath and collecting our courage before exiting the car and going up the concrete stairs towards the all-red-brick house adorned with four tall, white, classic Greek pillars on the front porch protruding upwards to the ceiling above.

The only thing that stood in the way of a peaceful night at home was one thing:

Courtney.

Acting more like a sergeant-at-arms guarding the Queens's castle, it was as if he knew telepathically how to time our arrival home each day, sure to be at his post just at the precise moment to put the fear of God in us.

The only way we could get by him was to shout to his dad inside, hoping Randolph could hear us. We'd holler out, almost begging him to bring inside his sociopathic son for a minute or two so we could pass.

Finally, after about three weeks of this, as the newly appointed man of the house, I knew I had to fulfill my husbandly duties and do something. In other words, time for Randolph and I to have a little man-to-man chat.

It was then that Randolph let me in on a little secret. His son had one flaw – more of a phobia. It turned out Courtney was deathly petrified of newspapers.

Just the slightest evidence of a folded-up wad of paper, be it even a tiny Post-it note, would do it. He would cow tail and race for cover, a spitting image from *Gone With The Wind*, where the Confederates soon began to realize they would be no match for the massive forces of their arch-enemy, Sherman's brigade, rapidly marching towards the city of Atlanta.

Only in our case, the oppressor was not those wretched blue-bellies from up north. Not even close.

Instead, it was much worse. Ours was none other than a five-year-old Shetland Collie – with a tail, a long-pointed nose, and four paws to match.

Now, I know what you're thinking. How could we be afraid of *that*? A little dog. A Sheltie, no less.

But we were – every inch of him.

The fact was that all 35 pounds of him could turn us into petrified little mice. He knew how to use his sharp, ricocheting bark to the utmost. As for the two of us, at least, it sure did the trick.

To our neighbors on our left and right and those across the street observing this drama unfold every weeknight, I could only imagine it must've been like catching a late-in-the-day soap opera ritual play out regularly at six o'clock. We must've resembled flies about to approach a Kentucky Fried Chicken bucket picnic runway, only to be redirected due to an oncoming fly swatter headed directly for us – and ready to send us into oblivion any second.

Only this fly swatter was in the shape of Courtney's salivating mouth and lethal reach.

Sometimes we'd be so frightened at his short sharp bark and quick lunging teeth, like when eyeing the first sign of lightning, in a flash, we'd high tail it back to our car and not dare look back. Of course, all this did was encourage him to bark even louder as if claiming victory, much like an alpha male Silverback gorilla pounds his chest when all his would-be rivals retreat.

Some nights we'd even be forced to camp in the car until way after dark, just praying for the slim chance he'd fall asleep, and we could gingerly scoot past him in time enough not to miss our favorite game show on TV, *Jeopardy*.

This pint-size beast had reduced the combined will of two grown college-educated adults to nothing short of that seen in the once-popular Disney flick, *Honey I Shrunk the Kids*.

That is until that day when Randolph spilled the beans.

A year or so back, daddy-dog became so annoyed by Courtney's unrelenting yapping and fearmongering that to try silencing him, he tossed a folded-up *Wall Street Journal* in Courtney's direction – not right at him -but close enough, hoping to shock and surprise the little mongrel. While at the same time, firmly saying, *"Newspaper!"*

Well for any of you who know dog breeds, you know that the Sheltie, while being an excitable creature for sure, is also extremely intuitive. Meaning Courtney got the message. And fast.

So much so that from that day forth, Randolph needed only to whisper even the word *Newspaper,* Courtney would dash away into an adjacent safe room and refuse to come out of hiding until he knew the coast was clear.

Armed with this new tidbit, it was a completely different war.

So, unbeknownst to dear Courtney, we thought we'd employ our latest weapon in our human arsenal the very next night upon arrival home. As usual, the little whippersnapper presented in full light brown and white fur battle fatigues.

We headed up the steps when only a few feet away from him now, Courtney began to lunge at us. But as he did, Annie, in her soft voice, laid down the gauntlet with one solitary whispering word -

"Newspaper."

In the blink of an eye, it was as if we had been given the keys to Mission Control and could override any previously programmed command. Courtney, at once, like any good soldier, obeyed the new order instantaneously. He sat, then laid down, his posture and face now submissive. And as to barking, zip, nada. There was no growl, no teeth showing, not even a licking of the chops.

As we peacefully walked by, it was like Annie and I were Lieutenant Colonels, and Courtney, a much lower-ranked Corporal, was forced to salute us until we made our way past him and onto the porch, then safely inside. Only afterwards, did he feel okay to proceed with his ongoing mission to intercept the next would-be intruder.

From that point on, our world changed – and I dare say, way for the better.

Such is how we must not be afraid to approach cancel culture. Or equally, the complicit media, who works in tandem with the Woke to put that same fear of God into the rest of the country.

How important it is to remember that, just as with Courtney, one's bark is often worse than one's bite.

I can't be sure what would've happened had we dared to cross Courtney's line in the sand. I do remember us feeling scared enough to pee in our pants. But would that spoiled child ever dare have bitten us? While Annie and I never had to find out, in retrospect, I doubt it. After all, what for him would have been the repercussions? Surely, he had some sense that it would not have ended well.

Like Courtney, the Woke will press forward until the moment they meet their match. One side or the other will have to back off. And like in any confrontation with a bully, when that happens, something intangible is gained: mutual respect.

What most of us want out of life, after a full and taxing day at work, school, or out running errands for the household, is to come home to a quiet place where we reunite with our family, share in each other's day, and gain strength so that we can have the fortitude to venture forth tomorrow, hopefully into some semblance of a predictable world.

It is a reasonable expectation to have.

But the over-the-top thunderous blasts from cancel culture have forced many to want to cower and hide. But this means only that what is needed in response is to embark on a more creative way to climb the stoops and arrive home safely.

Annie and I, with aid from Randolph, had to learn a more adept tactic.

What Jesus taught his disciples is relevant here.

There are two misdoings – one of commission and the other of omission. The latter happens when we fail to do what we know we should, pulling away from the struggle at the last minute only because of some spurious apprehension.

It is essential for us, who are the non-woke, to reflect on who is the captain of our team. Or, to say it more clearly, by referencing the story above, who is our daddy-dog?

Is it not the Lord of all Creation?

Much like Randolph, does not our heavenly Father know what can turn the scales the other way? By our prayers, contrition, and our putting on a spiritual ear of listening, He is competent to direct our response and collectively, in unison, counter counterculture.

The question for us now is whether will we remain satisfied sitting outside in our cars or decide it's time to bolster the necessary courage to claim back that which we rightfully possess: our lives, those of our children, and a future that centers upon faith and practice.

While our secret weapon may not be, as with Courtney, uttering a simple word to get the other side to drift away. Then again, maybe that, along with a laugh or two, is all it would take.

I might try it the next time I'm up against another yapping dog or anything else that refuses to let me respectfully pass.

Let's all practice it. Ready. On the count of three.

One...

Two ...

"Newspaper!"

Just Keep Laughing

It's hard,
anymore
I tell you,
knowing
whom you can trust.
A guy from my bank calls.
Tells me
I'm overdrawn.
But what if it's a scam?
I think to myself.
So, to be on the safe side
I decide I better
ask him a question.
"What are the last four digits"
"of YOUR social security number?"

If I still could have
children,
I'd want them
to be twins.
That way
I could tell

everyone I know
that once again
I finally got to have sex.
Twice.

I've got this old car.
A 2005
Buick Century.
Lilly, I named her.
Lilly and I
have this agreement.
Come morning
if I'm still
able to turn over
and get going -
so will she.

Rumor has it
UBER
wants to get into the elevator business.
Guess
they weren't satisfied enough
to have screwed us over
going horizontally,
they want now
to do it to us
going vertically.

Husbands ...
want to spend more time
making love
with your wife?
Then do this.
Build
in your bedroom
three closets.
One,
for you.
One,
for her.
And the third -
for each of
her 199 pairs of shoes.

Should
Trump
win a second term
Conservatives
are pushing the idea
to place his face
up on
Mount Rushmore.
Only the
stone carvers
will have none of it.

"How are we to construct all his hair?"
they argue.
"The sheer weight"
"could bring down"
"the whole monument."
What was Trump's reply?
"Then make me bald, I don't care."
"Just so long as I'm up there."
"... Well, do we have a deal?"

With
home burglaries
on the rise,
I taught myself
to sleep
with my eyes open.
Since then
not a single break-in.
But
my two cats
aren't all too happy with me.
Neither gets away
with half the stuff
they used to do.

I can't believe
I waited this long

to get one:
An electric toothbrush.
Each morning,
it's like
taking my mouth
through an
automatic carwash.
Almost as good as sex.
... An orgasm
for my teeth.

Have you had to
fly
International
lately?
You're better off
heading straight
into the Bermuda Triangle.
There I was
crossing the Pacific
on a 12-hour trip,
sandwiched between
two Japanese Sumo wrestlers.
My 140-pound body
started to shrivel up
like a
Sun-Maid raisin.
My cheeks

crunched in like
a blowfish,
sucking in air.
As soon as
the flight attendant
saw me
she rushed over
and shouted,
"Mister Holly,"
"what do you think you're doing?"
"What does it look like?"
I gasped.
"Trying to stay on the mat."

Wynn's Window to the World

When the cancel culture media crew tells all of us to stop laughing, then what?

Simple.

Keep doing it anyway until all their many shenanigans and those of the Woke come to a roaring halt.

Best to think of it like this.

Remember in middle school when the class clown started to lambast or make fun of someone to grab everyone's attention? Soon enough, though, those around the goofball came to realize how insulting he was; then almost in unison, those standing by turned it around and began laughing and making fun of him.

It was a surefire way to get the would-be-jokester to scamper away, his tail between his legs for having troubled and wasted everyone's time in the first place.

The same approach is workable still.

And here's how to get the ball rolling ....

Tomorrow, when you rise and proceed through your day, be sure to set your cell phone to jingle-jangle every hour, on the hour.

When it chimes ever so annoyingly in earshot, for those near you, tell them that you are doing it to remind yourself that you are of the *awake* generation, not the woke one.

Then, afterward, just for the pure fun of it, when you arrive home, why not check out what your horoscope for the day said?

It may just have read, "*Today will be the best day of your life.*"

Chapter Eleven

Dirty Old Aw

Which way back to Eden?

Traveling as I do, performing in various cities often on weekends, I like to stop in and visit a local church on Sunday mornings.

But my have things changed. And I'm not so sure I would say for the better.

I remember when churches used to be vestibules of hope, places of reverence, and where each week one could find a quiet place to meet up with God. Today, however, it's becoming harder to distinguish most assemblies of faith from attending a rock concert – a trend, I can only surmise got started to appeal to those not so inclined to participate in traditional worship.

I was living in Chicago at the time, when the first real mega-church such as this, *Willow Creek,* arrived on the scene. It was located in a far western suburb, South Barrington, Illinois, and exists there still.

It was here that the current state of "going to church" permanently took form. The thought was to make Sunday morning services "seeker-friendly." While this seemed to be a nice idea on paper; it was hardly one where worshiping and taking in the gospel's message could not help but become in time easily diluted.

Soon enough, church became that place people headed to when they needed to *feel* better about themselves, not necessarily to become a better self.

Fast forward to the first half of the 21st century.

Male congregants, not to be outdone by other fashion-conscious men, you see often show up now in casual shorts or jeans adorned at the top by *Tommy Bahama* shirts and below on their feet, *Docker* sandals. As for the women, it's nearly the same.

Only would these same folks choose to attend the wedding of a dear friend or family member dressed the same? I doubt it. Instead they'd likely put on their nicest clothes so to show respect and give honor to the bride and groom. If this is what we do for those we care about, doesn't it make sense that God deserve the same respect, if not more.

Today, churchgoers enter the "sanctuary", their cell phones, locked and cocked, while tucked up securely underneath their arms as if protecting a baby, the steam from Starbucks lattes rises from cups held in one hand, as a Krispy Kreme donut occupies the other.

Is it not fair to wonder, *What is it precisely that is providing these Sunday early morning risers comfort?* Is it God's Word or all the numerous trappings they are wearing and clinging onto?

Addictions embody many shapes, visible and hidden, but whatever form they take, you can be sure of one thing – ultimately they aim to distract us from giving and receiving what is most needed in that moment. True worship.

Back up on stage, a band plays ever so proudly while those out front in the audience flail their arms back and forth in flow to the music as if at a Major League Baseball game, orchestrating The Wave from one end of the stadium to the other.

I can't help but ask myself how this *Cirque du Soleil* extravaganza appears to those outside these four walls. If anyone of the Woke mindset were to ever become so moved as to seek spiritual rejuvenation, why in the world would they head to church when they could just as readily experience nearly the same in Las Vegas?

Furthermore, and perhaps even more to the point what would Jesus say if he happened to stroll by and make his way inside for a Sunday Worship Service, and witnessed this?

While I can't say for sure, I've got a sneaky feeling, upon first glance, after about five minutes what he might be inclined to do.

Leave.

A Telling Tale

Linus had his blanket, Dorothy, had her red shoes, and Joe Biden; he's had Jill. On the latter, thank goodness for the rest of us.

In each case– someone or something to rely on through uncertain times.

Now, as for the other seven billion dwellers on Earth central, we depend mostly on our cell phones to give us that extra sense of security, even going so far as to be sure to safely tuck them under our pillows each night before we dive fast off to sleep.

Ever since mankind first got bounced out of Eden, we've come to rely on some sort of contraption or another to get us through our day.

As for me, my need to settle my encroaching anxiety began very early on, not long after I exited the womb. I was just beyond toddlerhood, a little over three years old. What kept me settled was a small, folded-up pillowcase in which I took great solace.

I called it *"Aw."*

How I came to give it its name, I don't quite remember. What I do recall is that I would coddle it between my arms each night to help me fall asleep. I then would gnaw at it, sucking on it until it became drenched in saliva. The more ratty, smelly, and stain-soaked, the better. My mother and father soon got to labeling it *My Dirty Old Aw*. I suspect they threw in "dirty", hoping this might trigger a response from me to trash it.

But no chance.

It wasn't long until you'd see me carrying that stinky pillowcase wherever I went. By the time I turned three, *Aw* had graduated from being simply my nighttime companion but also my daytime one, too. All to my parent's chagrin.

They must've wondered if I was ever going to outgrow it.

Suffice it to say, that for me, laundry day was the absolute worst day of the week. After six days and nights of pillow torment I inflicted on *Aw*, Mom would be forced into having to give it a bath.

Each week when that moment came, she did her best to keep my mind on other things so as not to create in me side effects of dopamine-deprivation and withdrawal. She would find ways to carefully snatch *Aw* away from me without my ever catching on.

But soon enough what with the loud sound of the washing machine sloshing away in our southern Virginia basement, I knew there, and then I better head downstairs quick-like, much like a Geneva Convention humanitarian field inspector, to make sure *Aw* would survive another round of Mom's torture.

And for me to retrieve from her my drug of choice.

Only no such luck.

A couple of cups of TIDE made sure to take care of that. Once again, like countless times before, I would arrive on the scene too late.

Nor was I too fond of the idea that *Aw* would soon come out of that percolating white metal box of Mom's not only smelling like a rose but that she had the gall to then go about hanging it outside to dry on the backdoor clothesline, stretched out horizontally on clothespins as if it was being crucified.

I hated the sight of *Aw* hanging there stark naked.

In the little cubicle of my mind, such an action could only mean one thing.

All-out war.

As for those persistent annoying wash-cycle battle bombing raids, Mom often found it best to attack at pre-dawn, entering my bedroom when I still had sleep in my eyes and was least prepared for a surprise assault. Having snuck behind enemy lines, she'd tip-toe her way to the foot of my bed where she would steal *Aw* away from my clutches without my knowing.

As I saw it, given these combatant maneuvers, I was left with little recourse other than to return fire.

What I opted for was a Napoleon counter strategy where flanking your opponent without their knowledge was always a workable course of action. Once "my" pillowcase had been cleaned and folded, I'd purloin *Aw* from the scented linen closet where Mom had stashed it underneath a bulwark of towels. I'd be sure to schedule the ambush when she wasn't looking and be caught off guard. Then, not giving it a moment's thought, I'd reach for *Aw*, close the closet door, and make my getaway, hightailing it to my bedroom where I'd hide "him" between the mattress and the box spring.

Much like a NASCAR race car driver who eagerly awaits the green flag to venture down that first lap, I too could hardly wait for bedtime when, in complete darkness and solitude, I'd be able to suck, spit, and slobber away to my greedy-needy little heart's content. I'd yank that sucker towards the opening of my mouth, where my teeth and tongue would make sure to find their way to those cotton-white edges in no time flat.

And such was the story of my young life for nearly a year or more.

Undoubtedly, as the conflict raged on, I was determined to show the other side (my rascally adult parents) what they were up against. After all, I was in a fight for my life. To counter their schemes, when in their presence, and plain view, I'd make sure to slurp and lap up *Aw* in such a melodic, rhythmic pattern that even the conductor of the Mormon Tabernacle Choir would have been pleased with.

I kept this up continually until one day in late spring when Grandma and Grandpa Holly came to visit. They lived a few states away, so when they did show up, their visits always brought great delight to me. Grandma Holly, especially.

Little did I know on this particular visit, there was more there than met the eye. Grandma Holly – apparently having been made abreast about the 18-month-long war-of-wills – decided she should employ her powers of great persuasion to aid in my parent's goal of enlisting my ultimate and complete surrender.

Looking back at it now, I can't help but feel it was a joint conspiracy.

My parents, however, could've easily won this clash of egos quickly enough, and thus this *Battle of the Pillowcase Bulge*, had they realized one universal wartime axiom: whichever side has the most financial (and or for that matter spiritual) resources wins.

In this case, that was most certainly not going to be me.

With Grandma acting more like a certified court-appointed mediator, she came straight to the point in these Holly household peace talks. Forthwith, she came to the negotiation table and offered me ten dollars, right there and then, if I'd only exchange *Aw* for straight-out cash.

Ten dollars, are you kidding? This was great, I reasoned.

More to the point, I felt now in control of my own destiny. And who could argue with that? It was like my being the only contestant playing in a toddler's version of *Let's Make a Deal*.

While ten smackeroos may not sound like much now, back then, in the late 1950s, this would have been like fifty, no wait, one hundred big ones using today's monetary easing equation. For a young tyke to have that amount of money freely handed to him... oh my goodness. It was as if I had struck gold.

Just the sight of that fresh-smelling green bill tangling in front of my nose, the face of Alexander Hamilton staring back at me, I couldn't help but get goosebumps.

Yet, I wondered; if Grandma Holly were more than willing to forgo a ten spot, then maybe she could convince the other side to cough up a more significant amount. After all, releasing myself from this addiction most assuredly would come at great personal cost.

So, I countered by asking for two of those glorified greenbacks.

"Too much," the other side retorted.

After a bit more negotiation here and there, Grandma and I zeroed in on what would be the final terms; fifteen dollars.

So, I didn't get everything I wanted, I said to myself. Yet not bad for a few tense hours of peace bargaining.

Before I knew it, I had in my one hand not one, but now two of those folded legal tender papers. My eyes were bulging out from their sockets. Then Grandma went on to offer something else. She asked me if I'd be happier with something even better.

Who did she think I was, some dumb, stupid kid? Of course, I said yes.

Instantly, Grandma swept the two bills I was holding out of my hand and replaced them with fifteen round and shiny silver-dollar pieces.

Wowee!

To a little kid, not yet familiar with Piaget's theory of object obsolescence, MORE always seemed better. A half-pound of silver beats two pieces of thin, light green paper any way you slice it.

But then ... then came the moment of truth – giving up *Aw*.

I resisted at first, but I did it.

After which I thought to myself, *Hey, now that wasn't so bad*.

Only it would not be until bedtime later that night that the consequence of my decision made earlier in the day would hit home. Tucked underneath the covers, I, like a pilot about to engage the plane on autopilot, began to reach for *Aw* as I had done a hundred times before.

But where was he? I couldn't seem to find him.

Then I realized why. *Aw* was gone. I traded him away.

But for what? A few pieces of silver?

Like Judas, I had become the betrayer.

Only what could I have been thinking? Wasn't this my prime piece of real estate that I just tossed aside?

But then like a lightning bolt, and a snap of my little fingers, it came to me; maybe I could get *Aw* back. *Yeah, that's the ticket,* my tiny mind theorized. Then I'd possess both: Money and *Aw*.

But could I?

Didn't I a few hours earlier go ahead and sell off what would resemble Park Place in Monopoly? Who in their right mind would want to give it back? Certainly not my parents.

No, I deduced. It was time to come to terms with reality.

Negotiations were complete. All was signed, sealed, and delivered. *Aw* had become a casualty of war; and so, too, did I.

I don't mind confessing to you that the next several days were like going through pre-kindergarten detox hell. Yet, soon enough, as the emotional hold wore off, I discovered I could fasten my thinking on other matters.

And better things.

Of course, knowing I had that little piggy bank, sitting on the floor in the corner of my room next to me, bursting at the seams, sure helped. And what an incredible sound Mr. Piggy made when up and down I shook it.

Yes, I needed to move on; leave what was behind, and be willing never to look back. I must advance into the next era of my growing-up years and work to learn the art of contentment. Oh, but what an arduous task.

The Apostle Paul told his readers in his letter to the church at Phillipi that it took him years to finally unravel the secret to it all. He knew also it was something he could not teach others how to do; that no one could do it for you. It must be something one finds out on their own. He had only one word of advice, just as I discovered that fateful day as a youngster – **don't look back**.

By sharing this story, I've two points I need to make. The first is directed at those within the Body of Christ; the church. The other is meant for those attached to cancel culture. Though collectively, both embody the same idea.

How is the enactment of any of the ideas cancel culture sets before us going to bring contentment? They are not. Nor will they ever. Security? Forget about it. All lend themselves to tremendous heartache.

But what can one expect when the most potent force God has placed in the universe to keep societies and governments in check, that of the church, has gone AWOL? If there is an alternative way of living and being, those in the church have failed to articulate it. When attending church seems more like being seated at a sporting event, something is out of whack. The clear message of hope and forgiveness, along with moral living gets lost in translation.

Repeated in Scripture and seen time after time again throughout history is that which once the writer declared in II Chronicles 7:14:

> *"If my people, which are called by my name,*
> *shall humble themselves, and pray and seek my face,*
> *and turn from their wicked ways,*
> *then will I hear from heaven,*
> *and will forgive their sin,*
> *and will heal their land."*

The church's role is not to be the BFF to the world, Nor is it, as in years back, to be its prosecutor either, throwing out fire and brimstone from the pulpit. Rather it exists as a place, an avenue through which people, should they choose to, become equipped to escape from the many straight jackets that so entangle and can prevent us from breaking free from our addictions.

Only by seeking what God calls us towards can ever produce ultimate satisfaction. Aiming after anything else results in behavior more like that of a child unable to let go of sucking one's thumb.

Or in my case, chewing on a warn-out pillowcase.

Likewise, many confessing Christians have grown faint, lacking the ability to give sufficient devotion to divorce themselves from their mental crutches. I know I still have a few props I need to get rid of and I'm sure so do you.

If we dare to win over the hearts and minds of those within cancel culture, the church's mission must first be to show a resolve to return to what God asked of his creatures, way back at the beginning of time, in the land of Eden:

To love Him and to follow His precepts.

Then without a whole lot of fanfare, choose daily to heed His call, reverently and quietly.

Just Keep Laughing

Last month
I started
on this new diet.
All was going great
up until the 5th day.
That's when it occurred to me ...
What if my food gets lonely?

Home
alone
through the pandemic,
I took to speaking out loud
every thought I had.
To the point now
it's been
interfering with my dreams.
People
in them
are constantly
having to remind me
to shut up.

Yesterday
my horoscope read:
"From now on, things are looking up."
Man, that sure made me feel good.
That is until I read today's:
"Don't believe everything you read."

Why can't
all women
be more like
Dorothy
from
The Wizard of Oz?
One pair of red shoes
she knew was enough.

A funny thing happens
once couples retire.
Finally
the wife
can't wait for her husband
to leave and play golf.
It's three whole hours in her day
when she knows the house
won't reek of
Old Spice.

The longer
a couple stays married,
the crazier their arguments get.
Here's one
from my Mom and Dad.
"Don't you dare cremate me."
"I want to be put in an open casket,"
says Mom.
At which Dad returns fire with,
"Oh, yeah. Face up or face down?"
"I mean it,"
Mom shouts back.
"It's important I say goodbye"
"to all my friends."
To which Dad responds,
"You mean,"
"you're going to want to talk then, too?"

The next time
I have to fly
around the holidays,
I'm booking
a seat
on an
Amazon drone.
Not only will Jeff Bezos
guarantee me

same-day delivery -
you just can't beat
their door-to-door service.

I'm downright terrible
when it comes
to romancing women.
I'm so bad at it
one of my love dolls
even complained.
The manager
at the adult store
where I bought it
just called.
The doll's returned
and
is demanding
a refund.

Growing up,
I knew my mother
never liked me much.
She was constantly
inventing new ways
to get rid of me.
Once, she even got me this dog whistle
then told me

to go to the front door and blow.
When I did
all the dogs
in the neighborhood
would show up
begging
to bury me
in the backyard.

Wynn's Window to the World

Just growing up and making it to adulthood is hard enough.

So, it's understandable why many, once there, wish to secure a crutch or two to lean on now and then; in other words, those things we become disposed of and hard to let go.

It is a struggle all of us face.

And it is to this hunger-pain that the church must respond.

People will get out of bed on Sunday morning, even the Woke, if there is a place where they can go to hide out, even if just for a few hours, that provides solace and respite from a crazy, mixed-up world.

Ultimately, an intimate relationship with the creator of the universe is the only thing that can appeal to the imagination and give the human heart satisfaction and direction.

For those within the church what say we consider simply doing one thing, and that thing, very, very well: Focusing on sharing the message Christ came to Earth for:

To save us from ourselves.

Not even those within cancel culture could disagree with that.

Chapter Twelve

I Didn't See Anything, Honest!

The world's a stage.

I suspect there's a notion in all of us that says, "*Why not live and let live.*"

It is such an incredibly simple idea, yet it is this one formula that has helped to make America so special. And unique among all other nations. Needless to say, we are one big melting pot of some 330 million plus people, able to manage to coexist, even despite such various inclinations and doings.

In other words, no harm, no foul.

That is up until recently, given how cancel culture has sought to position itself front and center stage, above all other groups, promoting its wares to the point of drowning out all other philosophies and perspectives on life but their own.

Take, for example, the belief that one can switch one's sex for the other. And to do so by mere proclamation. A trend that appeared benign at the beginning of the movement, only a few years back, has grown to a fever pitch, making it so that even very young children are being taught they can choose which sex they wish to be ... then from then on, be it.

How ridiculous.

Eve suddenly didn't wake up one morning and hollered over to Adam, *"Hey Adam, guess what? Today, I've decided, like you, to be a guy. What say we go outside and toss the football around the garden before dinner?"*

God's plan was relatively simple: One man, one woman. Then to follow from them, a whole boatload of other-like characters after that.

It wasn't as if God said to Adam and Eve if you're not happy with whom I made you, fill out Form XY Chromosome, sign it, get it notarized by one of the Zebras, and bring it back to me Monday morning.

Procreation doesn't work this way.

... Uh, Oh.

I just caught the sound of the stage bell alerting the cast and crew that Act II is about to begin. I have a feeling it's going to be a humdinger.

Stay tuned.

A Telling Tale

Anyone remotely connected to the theatre is undoubtedly acquainted with the phrase, *the roar of the greasepaint, the smell of the crowd.*

Ever since my senior year, when I landed the lead role in a high school play and got my feet wet in "show business", I was hooked. One rarely gets over the sensation of those floodlights shooting down at you from above and being out in front of a live audience.

So much so that when I entered college, it took me forever to declare which major to choose to obtain my degree in, Marketing, my original plan, or Theatre Arts. At the end of my first year, I decided at the last-second deadline.

I loved both. More than that, I saw a future in doing both, as did many who knew my talents.

It was only by the toss of a coin that I went with Marketing. Had that silver dollar landed on tails, I'd gone the way of Mr. Shakespeare from the get-go. Yet while initially I chose the world of business to make my mark, I wanted to remain closely connected to the drama department. So, I ended up making Theatre one of my minors.

Fast-forward to early April of my sophomore year, where I was fortunate to have been cast in a supporting role in a play a troupe would take on tour over spring break. The play was *Doctor Faustus*, a tragedy created by Christopher Marlowe in the late 16th century. Our lead drama professor adapted the script, making the setting and language more up-to-date and resembling the atmosphere of the late 1970s.

From there, nine of us squeezed into a white rambling road-traveling van, a U-Haul in tow, carrying our make-shift portable sets, lighting and sound equipment, costumes, make-up, and suitcases. We were booked to the hilt all nine days, with fifteen Midwest shows spanning the week.

It was physically and emotionally grueling as we crisscrossed our way to and from Ohio, Michigan, Illinois, and Indiana. But what made this road adventure even more demanding was that all of us that week (as fate would have it) came down with severe colds, making the journey even more taxing. Not to mention all of us had mid-term papers and projects due the very first day back after returning to campus.

No rest for the weary.

How athletes seem to be the only live performers to gain university full-ride scholarships has always proved puzzling, given the revenue collegiate symphony musicians and actors also bring into the college coffers. If not immediately during a student's four years, later, most certainly, when star performers hit the big time either on stage in New York or on screen in L.A. where not knowing what to do with all the money they've accumulated they often choose to handout humongous donations to their alma maters.

Now, as to our classwork assignments, you must remember, that this was way back before there were PCs or laptops to rely on. And in that, I possessed the typewriter with the most bells and whistles, I was elected to bring mine along to generate our reports between afternoon and nightly gigs.

We all stayed busy between homework, shows, and catching up on sleep (when we could get it).

At each venue, not only did the actors perform, but we were also responsible for erecting the set each time before the show and striking it at the close of every performance. Our performances took place at municipal centers, mid-size community playhouses, a few large churches, and even a high school or two.

What got provided us in return for our gallant showmanship, given that we were all amateur actors and actresses, were two things: a hot meal each night, compliments of the venue, and separate dressing facilities for men and women to change in before showtime.

The whole week felt like we were characters in a *Hairy Potter* classic, making our way to what would become our next stop on our road to hopeful stardom. Or so we each pictured in our minds.

Young budding thespians from the audience approached us for autographs at the end of each show, in anticipation that one of us one day might make it to the silver screen... and they could tell all their friends I met so and so before they became famous.

As far as those nightly meals, most always, we could count on them to be beyond fantastic.

I often thought of it like we were all cowboys and cowgirls commissioned by some wealthy Texas rancher hired to bring in his herd over some long, dusty trail heading for Dodge. And where the only consolation for a long day of hard labor in the saddle was the delight of knowing Chef Cookie had rustled up on his backboard a buffet that not even the best of best chefs on the Las Vegas strip could conjure up.

Now, as for all the other want-a-be, Broadway-inspired actors on tour with me, Jen was the person I got along with the best.

Each night at the ringing of the supper bell, we'd band together, like Bonnie and Clyde, ready to pillage, loot, and ransack at our heart's content whatever items might be on those pot-luck smorgasbords, hauling back to our table another gigantic heap of meat, sauteed veggies, mash potatoes, and God knows every desert imaginable.

By mid-afternoon, we'd be so hungry; that come the dinner hour, we'd have eaten roast Armadillo if it had been served.

We were two typical college kids, ever so scrawny, with very little money to our names. So, those pre-performance meals often became our only nutrition ration for the day. And if God willed, Jen and I weren't about to let them go to waste.

While there was no love interest between us, we did go out on dates now and then. But no "benefits", as we both lived by a different code.

What cemented our friendship was two things. First, we shared a similar sense of humor. Very important to have when working together under any circumstance. Traveling in the van, we'd get to chuckling at something one of us said to the point that we couldn't control ourselves. Half the time, I'm sure the others, irritated to no end, wanted to toss us out on our rear ends.

Then second, there was this undefinable chemistry between us, which helped us play off each other when performing a scene on stage.

Even as freshmen, it was evident to the school's theatre heads that they had two young eager actors with genuine talent and willing to work hard to excel in their craft. And there was no way they were not going to take advantage of this to sell more tickets.

We knew how to make the most of our roles, not by solely playing our parts but by doing so in such a way as to make audiences feel as if they, too, were up on stage with us.

In other words, suffice it to say, that over those four years together, we each got our share of decent roles, though Jen undoubtedly won more than me, as she was truly a serious and gifted dramatic artist.

Honestly, I thought of myself as lucky just to share the spotlight with her.

Regarding our current billing and due to the melancholy dark nature of our play, the director had us all, both men and women dress up all in black. From head to toe.

In that, he wrote in several choreographed dance numbers all actors were required to wear black tights and solid-black pointe ballet shoes, including the men.

While viewing myself as a fully functioning testosterone-charged male, much of my presentation to the outside world up until then had been in jeans, a flannel shirt, sweats, and sneakers. In other words, your typical viral 20-year-old male. Transitioning from loose-fitting clothes to snug-fitting was more than challenging to get used to, especially those darn full-waisted leggings.

I remember having an exceptionally rough go of it for one performance. Maybe it was all those meals, and I had started to balloon up. Whatever, I couldn't get those nasty tights to want to go all the way up past my mid-section and lock in place to save my backside.

Plus, what made matters worse this night was that the dressing room provided us was anything but.

It consisted of just *one* tiny area, more of a medium-sized walk-in guestroom closet at best. Due to some renovation issues going on in the building that week, the venue where we were performing was unable to grant us separate rooms for men and women, meaning all actors needed to share (or better said, compete) and coordinate who would be in the dressing room at any given moment and to know which of us were occupying it, male, or female.

As we attended a well-recognized religious school, our director admonished us to be extra careful of the situation. He wanted to make sure, that when we landed back on campus, he'd have no trouble retaining his pre-tenure position and remain employed through the next dramatic art season.

He advised us that there be no hanky-panky nor any tricks played on other cast members. Of course, as you, the reader, know from an earlier tale, this just about killed me, as I always wanted to prank others.

Only this go around, the joke turned out to be on me.

Showtime was set for around 9 pm. There had been a blackout earlier that afternoon due to a storm, and just to be on the safe side, ticketholders had been instructed to arrive a bit later, making sure there would be lights on in the theatre, and that the show could still go on.

Beyond this, I don't recall much of the other logistical particulars. What I do remember, however, was when I was in the "dressing" closet I could make out the faint sound of Hawkeye Pierce's voice blaring out from a TV set in the adjacent room, which was easy, given the razor-thin wall separating us. And not only his voice but his other supporting surgical *M.A.S.H* members too.

It was one of those silly episodes where much was being made about holes in tents and how soldiers, from time to time, might get lucky enough to be treated the chance to peek in on the opposite sex showering.

Listening in, I was glad knowing nothing like that would happen to me. Or at least, so I thought.

That night we picked straws to see who would use the makeshift dressing area first, then next, and finally, who would be last. I drew the tiniest match, meaning I'd go in to change only after all others were through.

So long as I made it on stage on cue, so what?

Once inside the closet, I removed all my street clothes, socks, and even underwear, placing them on the hangers above my head. The men had special black-colored-like-jockstraps to put on that would match the dark leggings and costume. In this case, the strap, we'd put on over the leggings.

The leggings, being the first item to fling on, I reached for mine and began working them up my legs.

I had just about gotten them above my knees when suddenly, and without any warning, to my shock, the door to the closet swung open. There was Jen, who had busted in on the scene, perhaps returning to fetch some small item forgotten for her costume.

I'm sure she, like any of us, would have assumed that all other actors had already dressed and were in their positions, down on set, ready for the curtain to open.

All true, except for one actor.

Me.

There I was, no shirt, socks, shoes, or even a jock strap to my name. Utter nakedness, as Michelangelo's *David*. Only not him at all. Not even close.

Being small-framed, everything attached to me was equally small: ears, nose, fingers, you name it. Not the least of which also was that dangling modifier hanging down somewhere south of my belly button equator.

And, being in quite the relaxed stage I was in, what was drooping could hardly be found.

But how I wish, at that moment, if only I could have downed 1,000 of those little blue Viagra pills, that, in the eyes of Jen, what might stand out would be something truly remarkable and memorable, not something she'd try for the next 50 plus years to forget.

As soon as Jen surmised this awkward-moment-between-the-sexes landmine, she immediately began to push the door forward closed. And as she did, I heard her say, *"I didn't see anything, honest!"*

On first hearing those words, it was comforting. After all, maybe she didn't see anything. It did happen quite fast.

But then again, I knew what can happen when one makes a Freudian Slip. The truth lies somewhere slightly underneath the spoken words.

No, I thought, she did not see anything. Instead, she saw *everything.*

Only in my case, my everything was practically *nothing.*

Perhaps Jen was trying to be gracious; I didn't know. I only knew I felt terrible.

As the door shut, the only comeback I could even think of was, *"Give it time, Jen; I promise it will get better."*

As if "it" was sick or something.

But the fact of the matter was that the damage had already been done.

Yet to Jen's credit, she kept this *small* matter to herself, a secret between just us. To my knowledge, she never once shared what occurred with the other actors, or anyone else.

She honored me.

For good or bad, for large or small.

Honor is an underlying pin on what our country was built on – respect for one another. And an appreciation, too, of knowing the differences between right and wrong and factual versus fictional.

While "my little fellow" might not have been something to brag about, the person to whom he was attached to was, that fellow being – Wynn Holly.

As a result, because of Jen's mercy, I gave the best performance that night of all the fifteen I did on tour.

From there, Jen and I would forge an extraordinary relationship. We became stones sharpening stones. In her junior year, Jen went on to win Best Actor. Our senior year, I did.

None of us ever deserves to feel small. It is only among the Woke and cancel culture, that we are led to believe that an entire group of "other" people warrant such – mostly those of us who are unwilling to deny the existence of God and His plan for the sexes.

In the book of Ecclesiastes, the writer tells us there is a time for everything under the sun. There is a time to be humble and a time not to be. A time to be gracious, a time not to be.

I am willing to show in return – even to those who want to trample on my beliefs – honor, love, and grace to anyone, much in the same vein Jen exhibited toward me.

But unlike Capital One's cash back program, I do have my limit.

After all, this show called *Life* must go on.

Just Keep Laughing

I'm seated in this cocktail lounge,
ready to order my drink,
when suddenly,
the waitress
requests to see my ID.
"Wow,"
I said to her.
"Do I really look that young?"
"No, Mr. Holly,"
she said.
"But in case you keel over"
"from even this first one ..."
"my manager needs to know"
"where to send the bill."

If it's the thought
that counts,
I'm in trouble.
Mine
hopped a plane
somewhere east of Kazakhstan
about three years back.

Remember,
as kids
having invisible friends?
Mine
I still have.
Abby and James.
Only now
all they want to do is fight.
It's gotten so bad,
that neither will talk to the other
unless I'm around.
I hate it
when they
stick me in the middle.

Speaking
as a counselor,
the pandemic
certainly convinced me
of one thing.
Why God
gave us restaurants to go out to?
They save marriages.

As a boy
I used to love playing
Hide 'n Seek.
Today,
as an adult I still do.
Every time my friends and I
wind up
at Costco.

Come retirement,
men need a hobby
to occupy their time.
If I was still married
I know what I'd make mine:
irritating my wife.

Know what my problem is?
Even in my steamy fantasies,
women still find me to be boring.
The one I was with
in my daydream today -
three minutes into foreplay,
she hollered out,
"Got any mayonnaise?"

What's with
teen drivers today?
None seem to know
how to parallel park.
Their
skateboards
keep jumping
the sidewalks.

Someday, soon
I hope
to have a house on Mars.
It's the only place
I can think of
where not one Mormon
will ever dare
bike to.

I like staying up
to catch
the 11 o'clock weather guy.
He's the only other male I know
who gets things wrong
more often
than I do.

Don't think dogs are smart?
Two weeks
before our wedding,
my ex-wife's
insisted on a prenup.
Should she and I ever divorce,
he'd be sure to get at least
half my cat.

You have to feel
for kids
who grow up with lesbian parents.
Two mothers to have to please?
As for my mom,
she'd often forget who I was.
Even at the hospital
near the end,
her eyes shut,
I leaned down and whispered,
"Mom, it's me, Wynn. Remember?"
Know what she says back to me?
"Give me a hint."

Wynn's Window to the World

I feel it's fair to say that within the cancel culture movement, several seem to have lost touch with reality. Perhaps that may appear a bit harsh, yet for the ninety-five percent of us who are not woke, most feel it to be true.

To pretend something is so when it is not – that idea may come across as a promising premise to a Hollywood producer whose aim is to create a summer blockbuster sci-fi, but not for those trying to make it in one piece traversing through an already stressful world.

But more upsetting is to watch how the Woke react to those who disagree with them by chastening and excommunicating those who may see things differently. Shaming is not just something they've become good at; it is the only thing they are good at.

Even when those who get harmed the most are our children.

How, then, should those who are non-woke choose to respond? Unfortunately, cancel culture has made it so that there are now only two choices remaining: Stand one's ground or retreat for compromising is a word that is no longer in their vocabulary. What happens these next few years will be determined not by what those in cancel culture choose to do but by what you and I do.

Best to think on what confronts us now, as is true with all of life, as one grand-scale performance, in which we all must partake. There are no small roles nor an escape hatch or trap door near the back of the stage for one to climb down.

But quite frankly, I'm not looking for an exit ramp.

This time around, I'm hoping to earn an Oscar for my contribution. How about you?

Chapter Thirteen

Looking for Trouble

Laugher is always the better part of malice.

You've been living in a cave if you've not noticed it.

Anger – popping out within our society from every angle, nook, and cranny. But why?

I submit to you that one of the primary reasons is that our country has now way more people in the "have not" category than the haves. What's worse is that this discrepancy appears to be growing. Even more so, since COVID.

Nowhere is this more strikingly evident than when evaluating the difference among investors on the New York Stock Exchange – this country's main source for generating wealth aside from homeownership.

Less than only twenty years ago, the average price of the Dow Jones Industrials was shy of 11,000. Today, as of this writing, it is far north of 38,000 (an unbelievable number) and still climbing.

According to a 2019 report from *US News and World Report* (the year right before the pandemic), families in the top 10 percent of incomes held seventy percent of the value of all stocks, with a median portfolio of $432,000.

In contrast, the bottom 60 percent of households (most everyone else) with little left to invest after putting bread on the table held a mere seven percent of stocks – a striking disproportion.

As the adage goes, *the rich get richer, the poor, poorer.*

So, it's not surprising to see why the Woke has chosen to make use of this as a breeding ground to stir things up, even more so, through divisive conversation and subjective labeling.

In other words, malice. One group to another.

Nevertheless, this being said, the problem of income variance needs addressing. Otherwise, tensions will continue to mount – an issue, as a professing follower of Christ, I find in no way one to laugh at.

Only how best to rid ourselves of this enormous can of inequitable worms?

Certainly not by a re-distribution of wealth, as some impassioned reformists imagine. But by something way more concrete and stabilizing: **entrepreneurial opportunity**. At warp speed. The generation aged 40 and under is bursting with brilliant ideas. I know. I've counseled and advised thousands in my role at colleges throughout the USA. Yet many lack sufficient support to turn their passions into reality.

There exist way too many unable to chase after their dreams, all due to finding themselves financially strapped.

But when individuals are given back control over their lives, namely, the ability to secure for their families and themselves financial freedom (without the haunting prospect of over-the-top inflation, or worse a daunting recession) then all the rest of what cancel culture dreams up – be it pronouns, sexual orientation, critical race theory or whatever else – these will have far less likelihood to gain traction, let alone show up as a special segment on the evening network news.

My decision to bring this topic to the forefront, notwithstanding, feels right to do, though I know that doing so may unleash a firestorm. But the fact remains it is the 800-pound gorilla in the middle of the room that few on either side of the political aisle dare to seem to want to talk about.

I guess it is like my high school best friend, Jake, once remarked about me, *"Wynn, you're always looking for trouble."*

The simplest thing to do – for one who is a comedian like myself – would be to keep telling jokes. Forget jumping into the fray. Leave that to the politicians, preachers, podcasters, and gifted orators of the world, those types of folks.

But I can't. And here's why.

Just think of the things we used to be able to laugh at openly; only now they have completely been taken off the table.

If harmless-as-a-fly comedians are haphazardly being restricted on what can be said don't be surprised if regular conscientious folks, like most of you who have been enjoying this book, may soon have the Woke squadron knocking on your door, not long afterward, too.

Comedy club connoisseurs who once regularly attended shows now refrain from going, not wanting to catch a debate started by one in the audience ready to exchange tit for tat with the entertainer over the slightest particular word or phrase used.

Aside from crafting material to bring smiles to our onlookers, the task of any comic, or at least should be, is to point out the absurdity of what we, as men and women, say and do. In essence, all our many inconsistencies.

Good comedy seeks just that. Not so much to offend, but to shed light.

While chapters in the book have been geared primarily toward conservatives, I have approached this endeavor mostly with kindness, trusting that readers who may not always agree with me will also feel a tug at their hearts and minds as well.

Now that we've nearly reached the end, I hope you, the reader, have come away having experienced either one of three things. First, you may have felt like a part of you has been seated in a counseling office across from a trusted therapist. Second, you may have felt like you have been in attendance at your favorite Dry Bar comedy club, taking in a show. Or, third, you may have even imagined yourself seated in the back row of a structured, guided TED talk.

Whichever it has been for you, I'm pleased. It means I've come ever so close to accomplishing my goal – to inspire you to take action to counter counterculture, then to go about the work that will encourage and support economic influence for all.

Because without a resolve to do both, there soon may be very few avenues towards prosperity left and, worse, little leeway for any of us to laugh much else at anything.

A Telling Tale

My inability to evade trouble dates back to when I entered grade school.

Perhaps it was because I was one of the littlest kids in the class. Meaning I just felt the need always to be trying to prove myself. Regardless of the reason, when the teacher exited the room for a spell, you'd often find me, the little squirt of a fireball as I was, heading to the back of the classroom, hoping to hook in some would-be-challenger to a wrestling match, the goal to show everyone in this elementary school town I attended who was class King-of-the-Hill.

It was only after I ceased growing, just a few short years later, that I realized that if I was going to survive in this world, I needed to let go of the WWE take-it-to-the-mat routine and resort to using some other productive strategy.

Which I soon did.

Around my middle school years, I discovered I was a decent orator and pretty good at persuasion.

As a high school sophomore in upstate New York, I remember feeling ready to step into the batter's box and test out my newfound skills. The matter related to public high school students not being afforded the opportunity to hear both sides of the biological, *how did life originate* narrative. That is theories on how you and I came into existence.

Pretty much as it is today, 50 years ago, state-funded schools were permitted only to teach the strict organic side of things: Darwin and all of that.

On my initiative, I petitioned (or rather persistently annoyed) the district school board that *Creationism* should also be taught – or at least be stated as a feasible alternative. Substantiating my argument, I provided the necessary documentation to justify my case.

After much back-and-forth discussion and some months later, the Board finally acquiesced. They were willing to designate one entire class period within our 10th-grade biology course where Creationism could be the sole lecture topic.

Only now, the question for the Board was, who should they get who could be adept and qualified at giving the presentation? As you might guess, few teachers came forth to volunteer.

What was the decision the Board came to?

They elected little ole me.

But wait? What in the world was the Board thinking? I was not a certified teacher, not even close. I was a 16-year-old kid, for Pete's sake. On the other hand, I reasoned, at a public high school, just who else might they find who would be unafraid enough to risk giving it?

After I agreed to do it, the Board went on to inform me that students must be given the right not to attend the class that day. As for those who did choose to attend, none should be subjected to participate in the discussion, nor could they be tested on what material was shared. All okay by me. I was pleased simply to to have made some reasonable inroads on the matter.

Soon enough, the big day arrived.

And what happened? Students showed up in mass. The hallways leading into the classroom were jam-packed. Students wanted to be there, if for no other reason than the possibility of seeing my butt get hauled off to jail for going toe-to-toe against "standard scientific practices."

An hour and some change later, it turned out that no police came to put handcuffs on me. However, what did transpire was a lively debate where several students posed questions, and a truly democratic discussion ensued. For more than a full hour, both sides got to share their viewpoints, and where students listened attentively to one another.

Did I persuade any to believe in Creationism? Yes, But that was not the point. To my knowledge, my "side" nor the other was keeping score.

What I wanted, and why it was all so important to follow through with the presentation was the notion that no one side of the proceedings should be shut down or shoved under the rug simply because the other side feels it should be.

Why, might you ask, am I sharing this story? And, how is it relevant to *keep laughing anyway?*

Because it speaks directly to the situation in which we find ourselves today.

Like it was back then, people can not nor should not expect one side to give up ground without there being sufficient compulsion to do so. To imagine that cancel culture will roll over and play dead like a well-trained puppy dog is simply unrealistic.

And make no mistake about it. The rest of us who make up the non-Woke are the underdogs in this Dickens-like short story, fairy-tale plot.

Still, it is essential to remember that the lowly challenger often does win. And more times than one might think. David prevailed over Goliath; Churchill stayed off the Nazis. Had not both been able to counter with poise and persistence, the world that Jews and Christians now abide in would have looked much different. As would all the world.

And here we are again, our whole country stuck in a sort of *Back to the Future* moment. The prospects for the land betwixt two giant oceans, known as America, is up for grabs. What will Wikipedia, fifty years from now, write about the outcome? Let alone, even twenty-five years from now?

Do you need more proof that the underdog can win? Then try this one on for size, a Cinderella story from just a few short years ago. In the world of sports. NFL football, no less.

It was 2018. The Wildcard 9 – 7 Philadelphia Eagles went all the way to win the Super Bowl by the sheer gutsy play-calling of a tall, lanky backup quarterback named Nick Foles. No one could have imagined it.

The only way those scrappy Eagles pulled off the win and outlasted the world champ, the New England Patriots, was by pure tenacity. A belief in who they were as a unit and what could be achieved when hearts and minds were of one accord.

As 208 million viewers from home watched on their flat-screen TVs that Sunday afternoon in February, we saw those men in their scruffy green and white uniforms rally around their teammates. And as we did, we all felt goosebumps, seeing how each had a deep-seated feeling that a favorable outcome was their destiny.

As a counselor, working with clients of all shapes and sizes, unlike players for those Eagles, I've witnessed many succumb to the smallest of adversity, mostly due to a needless sense of shame and guilt over past failures or that nagging feeling they were inadequate.

Instead of countering those voices in their heads with gusto, they surrendered to "whatever will be will be."

We must all remember that on a human level, none of us is worthy in the eyes of a holy and all-inspiring creator. The book of Romans tells us, *"We have all sinned and come short of the glory of God."* Woke and non-woke.

Nevertheless, to allow one's lowliness of mind to permeate the conscience as to retreat from doing what is far nobler – would not this be the greater transgression?

While I know not all who read this book are called to be troublemaker bound as I am. Still, all must bear in mind and ask, precisely what is it we wish to leave to the next generation, namely our children and their children after that. Something will be left to them to inherit, both monetary and non-monetary. We as Americans all have a stake in what that should look like and can be.

Inside the hearts of those who proudly identify as sons and daughters of the *Most Highest I Am* is a spiritual toolbox and inside it are many gadgets to be plucked out at a moment's notice to counter this current encroaching harm.

One in particular works pretty darn well.

Laughter.

It is there to be utilized anytime. Anywhere, anyplace.

Just Keep Laughing

Of course,
I'm in favor of defunding the police.
Under one condition.
Each and every criminal
gets defunded first.

Remember *Metallica*?
That heavy metal-group
which once was all the rage.
To find out
what all the fuss was about -
I attended one of their concerts.
Three songs in
I shouted to the young girl
jumping up and down
next to me,
"I can't make out"
"a thing they're singing."
"Can you?"
"No,"
she screamed back,
"That's what makes them so good."

I've only one ironclad rule:
Never argue with an atheist.
What's the fun
in debating someone
who,
by all *their* own definitions,
don't believe
even they exist.

My teeth
said,
they'd each pay me
$50 bucks
if I
cancel my next
dental check-up.
I told them,
"Throw in a six-month supply
"of Kit Kat bars,"
"and you've got yourselves a deal."

Playing golf
last Friday
I realized
finally

what's been my problem?
Instead of
tossing my clubs
into the pond
on the 12th hole -
I should've been throwing myself in.

To save money
during these tight
inflationary times,
I've taken
to washing my clothes
and
showering
at the same time.
It's worked out great
save one thing.
I can't keep my ass
from banging up
against the sides
during the spin cycle.

I just found out
that our blood
travels through our bodies
some 60,000 miles
every day.

No wonder
most of us are so tired
all the time.

Yesterday
I passed by this restaurant.
Their marquee read:
Everything homemade.
I went inside
and gave the hostess a note.
"Sir, what's this?"
she asked.
"Directions to my house".
I said.
"Have the cook meet me there"
"in 20 minutes."
"Twenty minutes?"
she shouted.
"I know it's a lot to ask."
I added.
"Just tell the cook I'm old,"
"and if he wouldn't mind"
"giving me a good head start."

Have you
ever gotten your hand
stuck up deep inside
a *Motel 6* vending machine?
Just asking.

I can't stand
that *Google*
knows my thoughts
even before I think of them.
Oops,
I bet you
they just heard me
think that?

At breakfast
I like to watch ESPN.
Only lately
it's gotten to be so monotonous.
So, to pass the time
I came up with
a new sport:
spreading a little peanut butter
on the back
of the cat.
Not only
has it cured my boredom,

each morning
the dog's
got something
to look forward to.

Just to make sure
no one else claims my spot,
I posted a sign
on the cemetery plot
I just bought:
Reserved, Party of One.
This way, I figure,
when that day finally arrives,
and so I don't miss out
getting to heaven on time
I'll have DoorDash
deliver my last meal there, too.

Wynn's Window to the World

After the fall of man, to help his creatures cope, one of the best gifts God endowed humanity with was laughter.

It is a miraculous thing, isn't it? It empowers us with the ability to overcome tragedy, propels us to replace hostility with decency, and opens doors to have conversations with those who may disagree with us.

For in laughter, there is no malice. The two cannot coexist.

If you ever hope to keep the Woke's narcissistic intrusion into your daily life from growing, I'd advise this. Foremost and at every turn champion opportunities for entrepreneurship wherever you find them. Then realize, that to push back against the tide there will be moments when sticking your neck out a bit, will be required.

Then, finally, laugh - big, belly ones, too.

Laugh as if your life depends upon it. Because in these turbulent cancel culture times, it just might.

Then promise yourself one last thing. Whatever happens tomorrow, do yourself and everyone around you a great big favor: at all that is woke ....

Keep Laughing Anyway.